The Battle of
Upper Sandusky,
1782

The Battle OF
Upper Sandusky
1782

ERIC STERNER

SMALL
BATTLES

WESTHOLME
Yardley

Westholme Publishing, LLC
904 Edgewood Road
Yardley, Pennsylvania 19067
Visit our Web site at www.westholmepublishing.com

ISBN: 978-1-59416-401-9
Also available as an eBook.

Printed in the United States of America.

For Suzy

Contents

Maps

A gallery of illustrations follows page 56

Series Editors' Introduction

WE ALL HAVE HEARD and likely read about the big battles of the American Revolution. Names like Trenton, Saratoga, and Yorktown resonate in our ears. But what about all the smaller battles that took place by the hundreds, often fought away from but related to the bigger battles. It is the contention of this series that these smaller actions, too often ignored, had as much impact, if not more, in shaping the outcome of the American War of Independence.

These engagements were most often fought at the grassroots level. They did not directly involve His Majesty's professional forces under the likes of Generals William Howe, John Burgoyne, and Henry Clinton, or Continentals under Generals George Washington, Nathanael Greene, or Horatio Gates for that matter. Such smaller battles involved local forces, such as patriot militia and partisan bands of Loyalists, or at times Native Americans, mostly, but not always, fighting on the British side.

Quite often the big names were not there in such smaller-scale combat. Private Joseph Plumb Martin, writing in his classic memoir, recalled his fighting at Forts Mifflin and Mercer during November 1777. He and his comrades were trying to block British war and supply vessels moving up the Delaware River from reaching the king's troops under Sir William Howe, who had captured Philadelphia. Had they prevailed and cut off this obvious supply route, Howe might well have had to abandon the city. But no, they did not succeed. Superior British firepower finally defeated these courageous American fighters.

What bothered Martin, besides so many good soldiers being seriously wounded or killed, was not the failed but valiant effort to cut off Howe's primary supply line. Rather, writing thirty years later, what particularly irked him was that "there has been but little notice taken of" this critical action. Martin was sure he knew why: "The reason of which is, there was no Washington, Putnam, or Wayne there. . . . Such [circumstances] and such troops generally get but little notice taken of them, do what they will. Great men get great praise, little men, nothing."

While Martin's blunt lament is unusual in the literature of the Revolution, the circumstances he described and complained of are actually fairly obvious. Although often brutal, the smaller engagements too frequently have received short shrift in popular narratives about the conflict. Nor have the consequences of these various actions been carefully studied in relation to the bigger battles and the outcomes of the War for Independence more generally. Small battles accounted for the lion's share of the combat that occurred during the American Revolution. The purpose of this series is to shine a bright new light on these smaller engagements while also getting to know those lesser persons who participated in them, and grappling with the broader consequences and greater meaning of these actions on local, regional, and nation-making levels.

In the end, a more complete understanding of the Revolutionary War's big picture will emerge from the small-battles volumes that make up this series. If, as recent scholarship tells us, local history "allows us to peer deep into past societies and to see their very DNA," the Small Battles Series will do the same for the American War of Independence.

The surrender of Lord Cornwallis at Yorktown in October 1781 had little immediate impact on the fighting in the Western

Theater. Through 1782, and in some cases beyond, fighting between American Indians and expansionist white settlers continued with unabated ferocity. Redcoats and Continental troops were few and far between in the West, but with the assistance of British logistics and limited personnel, various tribal groups contested efforts by state militias and ad hoc settler attempts to push beyond the Appalachians at the expense of Indian homelands. In *The Battle of Upper Sandusky, 1782,* Eric Sterner has provided a succinct but vivid account of one of the most dramatic of the resulting encounters in the post-Yorktown West: the Indian rout on June 4–6 of a large contingent of American volunteers under the command of William Crawford, a close friend of George Washington. Crawford's Expedition had aimed at the destruction of Indian towns along the Sandusky River in the Ohio Country. The context of the battle was especially important. Three months earlier, Pennsylvania militia had wantonly massacred a hundred pacifist Moravian Lenapi and Mohican Indians at Gnadenhutten, also in the Ohio Country. The tribes who defeated Crawford along the Sandusky fought not only to repel invading Americans, but to avenge Gnadenhutten. As Sterner makes clear, the battle and its grisly aftermath—the Indians vented a terrible vengeance on Crawford and other captured Americans—was indicative of the brutality of the wider war in the West. Although major operations had ended in the East, in the Ohio River Valley Native Americans not only continued the fight for their homes and ways of life, but they actually held the initiative.

Mark Edward Lender
James Kirby Martin
Series editors

Introduction

War from the Bottom Up

IN 1806, EIGHTY-FOUR-YEAR-OLD HANNAH CRAWFORD mounted her favorite mare, Jenny, and set out for the banks of Tymochtee Creek in northwestern Ohio some 250 miles away, an area whites still knew as Indian country.[1] Her trip might have been remarkable simply for her age. But for all that, we would not likely know about it today had her husband not been famous. William Crawford was something of a minor celebrity on the American frontier. Not for his decision to relocate his entire family to west of the Appalachians when Pennsylvania was still a colony. Not for his business partnership with George Washington. Not for his service in four wars. Instead, William Crawford was known far and wide for dying horribly on the banks of Tymochtee Creek in June 1782.

It was an odd place for the sixty-year-old veteran of the Battles of Brandywine and Germantown to meet his end. Crawford's death was the culmination of a volunteer campaign against the Ohio Indians living on the Sandusky River, who had been waging an irregular war against Americans living in western Pennsylvania and Virginia for years. For three days in June 1782, volunteers from the frontiers of Pennsylvania and Virginia fought a battle against a force of warriors from several Native American nations encamped along upper portions of the Sandusky River and around a village known as Upper Sandusky in northwest Ohio. The allied tribes resoundingly defeated the Americans, whose sudden retreat collapsed into a pell-mell rout all the way back to the Ohio River. Several were captured, including Colonel William Crawford, who had fought in the French and Indian War, Pontiac's War, Dunmore's War, and as colonel of the 7th Virginia Regiment during the American Revolution. His captors tortured Crawford and the other prisoners to death, horrifying even their British allies and leading George Washington, who had known and worked with Crawford for decades, to caution any man against surrendering to Indians in the future.

The campaign and battle are largely overlooked today. They occurred after Yorktown, which had not appreciably affected the war west of the Appalachians. It was an American defeat and took place in northwest Ohio as opposed to the better-known frontier campaigns in Kentucky or New York. The campaign and battle also lacked some of the dynamic American personalities, such as George Rogers Clark, Daniel Boone, Simon Kenton, or Ebenezer Zane, who passed into frontier legend and mythmaking. If not for the brutality of Crawford's execution, the campaign might have simply been forgotten.

But for local participants, it was a watershed event. The idea of attacking Native Americans in western Ohio percolated from the bottom up, from the settlers of western Pennsylvania to local political leaders to the Continentals at Fort Pitt, who could do little more than sanction it. Continental authorities and forces watched from the sidelines. For Native Americans, the battle marked the growing independence of the Ohio tribes from both the Great Lakes Indians and the Iroquois Confederacy. Working across tribal lines, the Ohio Indian nations had amassed a multi-tribal coalition of Wyandot, Delaware, Mingo, and Shawnee that decisively defeated an invading American force, largely without the supervision of European allies. (A detachment of Butler's Rangers from Detroit was present.) Success contributed to the eventual formulation of the western Indian confederacy that defeated Arthur St. Clair in 1791 before General Anthony Wayne secured American victory in the War of the Northwest Territory at the Battle of Fallen Timbers, just seventy miles away. Yorktown might have brought major military operations on the coast to an end, but the American Revolution on the frontier continued.

During the Revolution, Continental authorities and state governments adopted a defensive posture along the upper Ohio River. The approach was meant to preserve a focus on the more critical coastal theater east of the Appalachians. It succeeded on that score but surrendered the initiative on the frontier to Native Americans and their British allies while leaving the Americans living in the area vulnerable to constant attack.

By 1782, frontier settlers on the upper Ohio, primarily in western Pennsylvania, could no longer tolerate the constant Indian raids. When local leaders proposed their own offensive to the Sandusky River Indian villages from which many raids had originated, Brigadier General William Irvine, commanding the Western Department, had little support to offer. At the same time, it was not apparent that he could stop them. Using what little leverage he had, Irvine crafted guidelines for the expedition and helped swing the election of officers toward William Crawford. Getting ready to meet them was a loose coalition of Ohio Indians, supported by a smattering of warriors from tribes in the upper Great Lakes, British rangers, and various scouts from Detroit.

Although their cultures and interests diverged, the two sides had more in common than they realized. Whether Native American or American settler, both were defending their homes, albeit with different strategies. The Indians faced an immediate threat against their villages; the Americans sought relief from years of brutal attacks. Decision-making was local, and the two groups clashed without regard to the broader strategic context. To call either force an army would be an overstatement. Each lacked an established organizational structure or command-and-control chain. Discipline was absent, as was the standardization of weapons, uniforms, and tactics. As a result, combat was fragmented. Men fought in clusters with their kin or neighbors, sometimes even facing off against one another as individuals.

Yet they were more than disorganized mobs. On the American side, most volunteers were enrolled in the militia and likely had been called up for service at least once. While not professional soldiers, they lived in a violent world and were accustomed to working haphazardly with one another to protect themselves, their families, and their communities. The volunteers were also aware of their deficiencies, which is why they sought assistance from General Irvine. Not only did he craft comprehensive instructions for the campaign, he discussed his operational concepts with the expedition's commander, Colonel Crawford. When they met, Crawford's position was not yet established, but Irvine helped swing the election of officers in his direction. The fact that Crawford was a veteran of several wars on the frontier and had commanded a Virginia regiment in the Revolution made him the most experienced field officer available.

His nearest competition was David Williamson, a lieutenant colonel in the Pennsylvania militia who had most recently presided over the cold-blooded murders of nearly one hundred Christian Indians on the Muskingum River. Williamson arranged and drove the idea of a volunteer campaign to Sandusky to its fruition. Symbolically, Crawford and Williamson represented the yin and yang of managing violence on the frontier, from organization and professionalism to ad hoc bodies engaged in indiscriminate bloodletting.

Things were similar for the Native Americans, with a few notable differences. The involved Indian nations had long experience of raiding warfare, and it is likely at least some of the senior leaders had as much, or more, experience leading men into battle as Crawford. But many of those battles had been opportunistic and indiscriminate surprise attacks against unprepared civilians. The Wyandot had not faced an American incursion during the war, but the Delaware had dealt with invading armies during Dunmore's War. After finally siding with the British in the Revolution, they faced an American invasion largely foiled by weather and flooding. The Shawnee had engaged substantial frontier armies during Dunmore's War at the Battle of Point Pleasant and then a major invasion of militiamen from Kentucky County, Virginia, in 1780. While more experienced, they were late to the Battle of Sandusky. The Ohio Indians too had their more veteran advisers. British Indian agent Matthew Elliott and officers leading a small contingent of Butler's Rangers came down from Detroit to fight with them, but they could no more control Indian leaders than Irvine could order about the American volunteers.

In other words, the men who fought on both sides were amateurs largely untrained in the art of war, but they were not neophytes in either military operations or combat, due at least in part to the near-constant state of violence on the frontier. They were entirely representative of the people who fought the larger engagements that took place west of the Appalachians during the war.

At the end of the day, the campaign against Sandusky reflected the nature of the American Revolution on the frontier. Whether Native American or white, it was a bottom-up conflict, fought by locals for their own reasons, under their own leaders, with their own resources, and often without decisive guidance from national authorities.

ONE

War on the Upper Ohio

THE AMERICAN COLUMN SPLASHED across the Ohio River at Mingo Bottom on March 10, 1782, leading some eighty horses rattling with the tools, pots, pans, knives, shovels, hoes, and household goods seized from Native Americans living along the Muskingum River. It was a motley group, lacking the discipline, uniformity, and organization associated with military units in the East, but it represented the typical way frontier settlers banded together to fight the American Revolution. Most of the riders were in a jubilant mood, congratulating themselves for conducting a successful campaign against Indians they held responsible for aiding, abetting, or participating in raids against their farms and villages across western Pennsylvania and northwestern Virginia for years, resulting in theft, kidnapping, murder, and mutilation of men, women, and children.[1] Many of their views were well-rooted in personal experience and the memories of acquaintances, friends, and loved ones they had lost.

They left behind three well-ordered European-style villages all reduced to smoking ruins, the surrounding fields trampled, and the charred bodies of over ninety men, women, and children lying among the embers and ashes, already being picked over by animals. The Americans, led by Lieutenant Colonel David Williamson of the Pennsylvania militia, had entered the towns of Gnadenhutten and Salem under the guise of a peaceful intent.[2] Over two days, they rounded up the residents and collected them at Gnadenhutten, separated them from anything that might be used for self-defense, bound them, bludgeoned them to death, scalped the bodies, and burned the buildings that held them. The Native Americans, mostly members of the Lenape nation and also known as the Delaware, were converts to Christianity and had adopted many European traditions, ranging from their farming techniques and family life to manner of dress and worship. They spent the bulk of the American Revolution trying to navigate the waves of violence that washed across the frontier from both the Americans to the east and hostile Indians to the west, attempting to remain neutral in the conflict. They probably knew many of their attackers personally, yet the Americans killed them in cold blood just the same. Simply, they had arrived at a point in their thinking where all Indians were enemies to be killed, no matter how peaceful those Indians might be. Such was the nature of warfare on the frontier: brutal, intimate, and dehumanizing.

Before the column crossed the Ohio, at least some of the men resolved to recross and conduct an offensive against the Indians living along the Sandusky River, about one hundred miles to the west. The plan was to assemble six hundred men at Mingo Bottom on March 18.[3] The "victory" they thought they won had whetted their appetite for bloodshed on a still larger scale.

It was too much to expect the raiding party from Gnadenhutten to reassemble just eight days after crossing the river, but time, profit from the booty seized, and a return home did not satisfy the grassroots desire to defend their homes by taking the war to, and indiscriminately killing, Indians. On March 24, a body of men attacked a settlement of friendly Delaware on Killbuck's Island, just outside Pittsburgh. These Native Americans had relocated to the area for safety from hostile tribes farther west, including fellow British-aligned Delaware and Wyandot along the Sandusky River. Of those killed, two held commissions as captains in American service. The rest fled for the relative safety of Fort Pitt.[4] When their pursuers reached the gate, the raiders threatened Colonel John Gibson, commanding the fort at the time, accusing him of being too friendly to the Indians.[5] Some even threatened to hang him. The victims had been under the protection of a Continental guard, which Brigadier General William Irvine, commander of the Western Department at Fort Pitt, suspected of helping the attackers.

IRVINE'S SUSPICIONS REFLECTED a larger problem. The state of affairs among the Americans in spring 1782 was muddled and unsatisfactory. The Continentals distrusted the militia; the militia distrusted the Continentals; and the civilians in the area were unhappy with both. At the beginning of the war, Virginia and Pennsylvania both claimed the area around Pittsburgh and created duplicate and overlapping county governments and militia systems. In practice they had sorted the issue out by 1779, but local residents often disagreed with the outcome. So, state loyalties were not clear cut when it came to recruiting and militia service. Through seven years of war, no civil or military authorities had been able to secure the frontier and prevent Indian raiding parties from striking well south and east of the Ohio River. British-allied Native American war parties had raided across the frontier from the Allegheny River to Kentucky nearly at will. Collectively, the raids were every bit as brutal as the massacre at Gnadenhutten, usually resulting in theft, mutilation, kidnapping, slavery, and murder.

Continental military authorities acknowledged the problem. Irvine's predecessors had pleaded with the commander in chief, General George Washington; the Continental Congress; and state authorities for support to conduct an offensive against Detroit.

Little had been available, and the Continentals only made it to the Muskingum River, a few miles north of Gnadenhutten. There they built a fort in fall 1778, only to abandon it in early 1779.[6]

After the bulk of the Delaware Indians sided with the British, Irvine's predecessor, Colonel Daniel Brodhead, conducted a punitive campaign against them in April 1781. The farthest he reached was the village cluster of Goschgosching at the fork of the Muskingum River. The campaign revealed some of the tensions dominating the American side of the war on the upper Ohio River. Brodhead relied on 150 Continentals and a like number of local militia, arranged into four companies. When one militia company threatened to mutiny, march on Gnadenhutten, and burn the town, Brodhead and Colonel David Shepherd of the Ohio County, Virginia, militia had to face them down with loyal troops.[7] Brodhead eventually reached Goschgosching, burned the parts of the town on his side of the river, and took a few prisoners. While Brodhead spoke with one chief who had approached the colonel under a promise of security, a militiaman rushed up and tomahawked the chief midsentence. Later, on the way back to Fort Pitt, the militia murdered Brodhead's prisoners in the dark. That fall, Washington relieved Brodhead of command after conflict between the colonel and local authorities became intolerable and charges were levied against the colonel's management of public funds. (He was later acquitted.) Colonel John Gibson of the 7th Virginia took over on an interim basis.

When Irvine arrived in November 1781, he found the Continentals at Fort Pitt understrength, ill supplied, and mutinous. Wider affairs across the department were generally in chaos. He responded by reorganizing the two regiments there into two companies each and sending a number of officers home. Then he complained to Washington: "I never saw troops cut so truly a deplorable, and at the same time despicable, a figure. Indeed, when I arrived, no man would believe from their appearance that they were soldiers; nay it would be difficult to determine whether they were *white men*."[8] Irvine spent the winter working to rectify the situation, arrange pay, restore order, and improve Fort Pitt's crum-

bling defenses. He spent much of the time in Carlisle or Philadelphia and made some progress, admittedly by hanging a few soldiers convicted of mutiny, but relationships with the locals
remained fraught. He lacked the resources to defend his own
forts, much less patrol the frontier or pursue raiders. The locals
noticed. Despite Irvine's efforts, the Continentals were still not
up to the task, and locals constantly berated Continental soldiers
and officers. The noncommissioned officers of the 7th Virginia
took the extraordinary step of putting their concerns in writing
to Irvine directly, noting they had been "upbraided by the country
inhabitants for our fidelity—they calling us fools, cowards and a
set of mean fellows for staying without our pay and just dues."[9]

Irvine estimated he needed roughly 950 healthy soldiers just
to garrison and patrol the frontier during the normal raiding sea-
son, April to October. He had about two hundred available at Fort
Pitt. (He thought Westmoreland County could provide one thousand militia and Washington County two thousand.)[10] When ap-
pointing the brigadier general to command at Fort Pitt, Congress
had authorized Irvine to call in "such aids of militia as may be
necessary for the defense of the post under his command and
protection of the country."[11] So, on April 5, 1782, he met with the
county lieutenants or their deputies from Westmoreland and
Washington Counties, Pennsylvania, and Ohio County, Virginia,
to discuss strategy. Westmoreland County had suffered significant
militia losses eight months earlier when reinforcements it sent
down the Ohio River under the command of County Lieutenant
Archibald Lochry were ambushed, killed, or captured near pres-
ent-day Cincinnati. Lochry's replacement, Colonel Edward Cook,
and his sublieutenant, Colonel Charles Campbell, represented
the county at this strategic conference.[12] Colonel James Marshel
from Washington County was unavailable, but his deputy, Colonel
George Vallandingham, attended on his behalf. Lieutenant
Colonels David Williamson and Thomas Crooks, as well as Majors
James Carmichael and James Edgar also joined. The stalwart
Colonel David Shepherd and Major Samuel McColloch were
there from Ohio County.

The militia officers agreed on a twofold strategy. Irvine would garrison Fort Pitt and Fort McIntosh on the Beaver River with his Continentals while the militia would form "flying companies" that remained in constant motion along the frontier, looking for signs of Indian incursions and prepared to give pursuit at a moment's notice. Westmoreland County contributed 65 men in two companies, and Washington County dedicated 160 men. Colonel Shepherd of Virginia could promise nothing until he received authorization and guidance from Richmond.[13] It was a defensive strategy entirely inadequate to the task as Irvine saw it, but the best military authorities felt they could do at the time.

THOUGH IRVINE'S PRIMARY INTEREST was defending the frontier, a proposed campaign into the Ohio country came up. Irvine heard word of it in March but could determine few details.[14] Under a separate cover, Colonel Marshel wrote the brigadier with additional information. Williamson delivered the letter at the conference. In Marshel's view, Williamson was the prime mover behind an expedition to Sandusky and had set aside a substantial amount of flour to supply it. While he expected to raise a large body of troops from Washington County, Williamson also assumed some might be raised in neighboring Westmoreland County. Most importantly, Marshel observed, "The people in general on the frontiers are waiting with an anxious expectation to know whether an expedition can be carried against Sandusky early this spring or not. I could therefore wish that Colonel Williamson would be countenanced in this plan if with propriety it can be done."[15] (Surprisingly, at the same time Marshel indicated Williamson would help supply a campaign against Sandusky, he complained to Irvine that he could not supply militia called up for service to garrison or patrol the frontier.)[16]

Irvine neither countenanced nor rejected Williamson's proposal. Instead, he ordered Captain Uriah Springer of the Virginia Line across the Ohio to scout the land in the direction of the Sandusky River with three whites and three Indians. Understandably, the Indians were skittish about the trip. After all, they had been attacked by their so-called white allies around Pittsburgh and were headed toward the British and their hostile Indian allies. Whether tipped by Springer or someone in his party, Continental authorities suspected one of the assigned Indian scouts, John Eels, of intending to betray Springer and his men. On April 11, Irvine ordered a board of inquiry, which concluded that Eels had solicited other Indians to defect with him. If that happened, the board further concluded that Eels would reveal Springer's location and intentions. It recommended death for treason. Irvine confirmed the recommendation and had Eels shot on April 12. Springer's party still departed the fort, but it returned prematurely having learned very little.[17]

In the first week of May, the locals again raised the issue of marching to the Sandusky. Colonel Marshel sent Irvine another note announcing that the sentiment in Washington County was all in favor of the expedition and that he believed they could raise sufficient forces. On May 7, a delegation from the area, including Dorsey Pentecost, a member of the Supreme Executive Council of Pennsylvania, approached the general again and urged his support for it. They also seemingly deferred to his judgment.[18] Irvine was reluctant to treat the idea as an official proposal from the Pennsylvania government, which it was not. Instead, he wrote Washington, "A number of the principal people of this country made application to me, about two weeks since, for my consent to their collecting a body of volunteers to go against Sandusky."[19] In other words, Williamson had proposed an ad hoc group for one specific purpose. Marshel had endorsed the idea, but deferred to Irvine. Then local political leaders put the idea to him while still seeking his approval. Colonel Marshel and Colonel Cook reportedly offered to exempt volunteers from two months' militia service—which would count against any militia call-ups Irvine prodded Pennsylvania authorities to make.[20] So, while Marshel would not call up the militia for the campaign, his advocacy made it a quasi-official event at the expense of the militia resources available to Irvine. Even so, local recruiters did not wait for a formal response from Irvine and began putting up recruiting posters in April looking for volunteers.[21] They named May 20 as the rendezvous date and Mingo Bottom, on the *northern* side of the Ohio River, as the location. Irvine might well have no choice but to bless the offensive.

THE MURKINESS OF THE SITUATION lies in some of the quirks of Pennsylvania's military traditions. Whether as a colony or state, Pennsylvania did not have a history of creating and sustaining military forces. The Penn Family Proprietorship preferred to promote its security through a complex mix of diplomacy and land purchase. It had the advantage of working through the Haudenosaunee, also known as the Six Nations or Iroquois Confederacy. The Haudenosaunee claimed suzerainty over the Native Americans living in territorial Pennsylvania, so it was no great leap for the Penns and the Haudenosaunee to collude to transfer territory in Pennsylvania from subordinate Indian nations to the Pennsylvania government in exchange for payments. The system worked well enough at maintaining peace, but it left Pennsylvania woefully unprepared when it failed.[22] The outbreak of the French and Indian War found the colony with no standing militia law. Even then, it did not pass a temporary one until long after France and its Indian allies began raiding the Pennsylvania frontier. To protect themselves, grassroots groups began forming their own associations that functioned as a quasimilitia. Participants became known as Associators, and these groups often provided the backbone of military power for the Committees of Safety that sprang up as the Revolution began.[23] Thus, military forces in Pennsylvania had a recent history of being organized and commanded from the bottom up.

In 1777, Pennsylvania finally passed a militia law automatically enrolling all white males eighteen to thirty-five. It established a county-based system with a county lieutenant and sublieutenant responsible for military affairs, ranging from organizing military districts from which a battalion would be raised to calling up a group of men for operations based on, theoretically, a predetermined class. These were civilian positions, but the individuals holding them held the military rank of colonel and lieutenant colonel.[24] Through 1779, county lieutenants would call up an entire class, or several, to meet the needs of the county and to serve with the Continental Army for a period of time. These were the militia that George Washington and other Continental officers were so fond of criticizing. Farther west, however, county lieutenants exercised their authority and responsibilities more loosely, often limiting a called-up militia class to serve locally by garrisoning forts, patrolling trails, and pursuing Indian raiding parties. That trend accelerated after 1780.[25] These were the kinds of military forces that Continental officers in Pittsburgh and county authorities relied on for frontier defense. Such deployments could last for months, keeping the militia class away from homes, farms, and trades. Being absent from home, of course, left isolated farms even more vulnerable to Indian raids. So, being called up for lengthy service was not popular with most frontier settlers. Westmoreland and Washington Counties relied on called-up militia classes to perform the agreed upon functions at the April 1782 conference. But the unpopularity of such service explains the paltry turnout for Irvine's priorities and the popularity of a short-term raid.

THE IDEA FOR A CAMPAIGN to Sandusky predated the Gnadenhutten massacre and the proposal from Washington County's political and military leaders. Colonels Brodhead and Gibson had argued over such a proposal in fall 1781, particularly the question of who should command it. As usual, the proposed Continental-led campaign came to naught. Frustrated with the failure of the Continentals and, for that matter, the militia to stop Indian raids, locals began proposing their own attacks on Native American communities. For example, Colonel Marshel rejected a request from Irvine to bolster Fort Henry's defenses at Wheeling on Virginia's Ohio River border, informing the general, "I can not comply with your requisition of engaging a number of men for the defense of Fort Wheeling, as I am heartily tired out with volunteer plans."[26] Still, an offensive made sense. The frontier war was not usually a contest between organized armies; it was a never-ending series of skirmishes and raids between Indian war parties and groups of farmers, hunters, and traders who could be cobbled together at any given moment. Settlers on the frontier experienced the war as noncombatants engaged in self-defense, clustered in private blockhouses or fortified villages, and ad hoc parties of neighbors assembled to pursue groups of Indian raiders. Enlarging and focusing those ad hoc groups to take the war into Indian territory was a natural step. Such volunteer groups were short term, less bound by the limitations of militia rules, did not take men away from their homes, farms, or businesses for long, and sometimes resulted in booty. For people living on the frontier, they were preferable to months-long duty garrisoning forts or patrolling Indian trails.

The distinction between militia and nonmilitia operations was subtle but important. When Irvine informed Washington of events at Gnadenhutten, he used the phrase "country people" to describe the American attackers.[27] By 1782, the American Revolution on the upper Ohio frontier was war from the bottom up. It would no longer be directed from the top down. On the American side, the initiative had passed from the Continentals and the militia to the "country people." Now they proposed to take the field again and march all the way to the Sandusky, this time with explicit support and leadership from the militia and the Continentals. The April recruiting efforts hinted that they might proceed without it.

FOUR RATIONALES WERE OFFERED for the campaign against Sandusky in April and May. Early historians who lived in the area and sought to tell the frontier story in the first few decades of the nineteenth century reported that some frontier settlers wanted to continue with the destruction of Moravian settlements in the Ohio country.[28] (In fall 1781, British-allied tribes in western Ohio had forcibly relocated Christian Indians living along the Muskingum to, for lack of a better word, reservations along the Sandusky River. The Native Americans killed along the Muskingum in March returned primarily to gather food and supplies from their old homes and farms to feed their brethren still trapped on the Sandusky.) C. W. Butterfield, who wrote the first serious history of the campaign, traced that idea to historians from the Church of the United Brethren, more widely known as the Moravian Church, which had so recently lost its Indian parishioners on the Muskingum and feared for the safety of those remaining on the Sandusky. Unfortunately, Joseph Doddridge, who grew up among veterans of the frontier wars and eventually transformed local lore into one of the first regional histories, accepted the church interpretation of the campaign's origins. Subsequent frontier histories followed Doddridge on that score. So, the notion persisted.

Butterfield found no compelling evidence other than assertions by the Moravian Church that the campaign was aimed primarily at the Christian communities.[29] His analysis holds up well. Colonels Brodhead and Gibson of the Continental Army had discussed a Sandusky campaign before the Gnadenhutten massacre. In winter 1781-82, Irvine inquired whether it might be possible to build a wagon road from Sandusky to Detroit, indicating he was thinking more grandly about a campaign to the region.[30] Subsequent memoirs and narratives by volunteers specifically rejected the notion of another campaign against Moravian Indians, perhaps stung by the association with Gnadenhutten. For that matter, destroying refugee Moravian settlements on the Sandusky would do nothing to improve security. People living on the frontier knew that any campaign to the Sandusky would run into the heart of the militant Wyandot and Delaware tribes, both openly and avowedly hostile. Any campaign to northwestern Ohio might well meet with substantial armed resistance. It would be necessary to destroy or displace the Wyandot and Delaware, not simply slaughter the remainder of the Christian Moravian Indians.

Of greater value was Doddridge's more thorough examination of frontier motivations, in which he found a broader animosity against all Indians, exacerbated by years of relentless brutality during the war. He found that the war had "debased a considerable portion of our population to the savage state of our nature." He considered a thirst for revenge fundamental to that "savage state of our nature" and noted that every family had lost relatives and witnessed murders in the area during the war. So debased had they become that a war of extermination was a natural outcome.[31] In short, a campaign to the Sandusky was an opportunity for revenge.

A second train of thought also guided the origins of the campaign. It was common practice, what we might call doctrine today, to attack Indian villages as a way of driving tribal communities away from their means of sustenance. By raiding villages, destroying crops, and preventing hunters from acquiring meat, colonial—and then American—authorities could reduce tribal communities to subsistence living and preempt attacks on white settlements. In the American Revolution, this had the added strategic benefit of forcing Native Americans into greater reliance on storehouses in Canada. When George Washington ordered Major General John Sullivan to invade Iroquois territory in 1779, it was with the expectation that the general would drive the Indians away from the New York frontier and destroy their sources of grain, making them a burden on the British.[32] Colonel Brodhead, ordered to make a supporting foray up the Allegheny River, was concerned that supply shortages might so delay his campaign as to enable the Indians to harvest and carry off their corn crops.[33] When he finally returned from the campaign in September, Brodhead was confident the successful foray would provide some relief to frontier settlers and villages in several counties in western Pennsylvania.

In late 1781, that was still a commonly accepted principle for waging war on Native Americans. William Moore, president of the Pennsylvania Supreme Executive Council, noted to General Irvine that "it has been suggested to the general assembly that the best and perhaps cheapest means of protecting the frontiers will be found in the invasion of Indian country."[34] People living on the frontier understood this. Even as early historians accepted and popularized the notion of a revenge-driven campaign in a war of extermination, they acknowledged that most of the men who volunteered for the campaign truly wanted to take the war to the Wyandot who called the Sandusky home as a means of relieving their own communities from Indian raids.[35] One motivation is not incompatible with the other.

A third rationale driving the campaign was Brigadier General Irvine's desire to bring the Indians to battle, not merely to drive them away from the Sandusky River. An advance on the Wyandot, who were closer to Detroit than Pittsburgh and had not suffered the consequences of retaliation for their attacks across the Ohio, might force them to take a stand. Certainly an American success would undermine Indian loyalty to Britain, which would have failed to provide protection. He wrote Washington, "we find, by experience, that burning their empty towns has not the desired effect. . . . They must be followed up and beaten, or the British, whom they draw support from, totally driven out of their country."[36] The difficulty of bringing Native Americans to pitched battle led Irvine to focus on the British, which meant seizing Detroit. George Rogers Clark had drawn much the same conclusion in Kentucky. He and Colonel Brodhead sought to coordinate a campaign in 1781, but it came to naught. The passage of time had not changed the fundamental analysis, and Irvine proposed leading a force of seven hundred to eight hundred continentals and a thousand militia on a rapid march to Detroit to seize the fort by storm in late summer 1782, when the ground was dry and would facilitate a rapid advance. Washington did not immediately reject the idea and blessed Irvine's plans to seek support, particularly resources, from the Pennsylvania government and the Continental Congress. So Irvine traveled east, leaving Colonel Gibson in command during the winter.

Irvine's efforts failed. On March 8, while Williamson's men were slaughtering peaceful Indians on the Muskingum River,

Washington finally sent Irvine the bad news. Resource constraints meant that "offensive operations, except upon a small scale, cannot just now be brought into contemplation."[37] Detroit was off the table, but that did not invalidate Irvine's belief that the Indians had to be "followed up and beaten." So Lieutenant Colonel Williamson arrived at the April conference with Colonel Marshel's letter at an opportune moment. If a campaign against the Sandusky villages successfully brought the Indians to battle and defeated them, the frontier might still find some lasting relief from attacks. Though they came from different directions, the "country people" and the Continental general arrived at close to the same place. Continental Brigadier General William Irvine would support local efforts to make good on the resolve of the Gnadenhutten raiders to attack the Indian villages along the Sandusky River, from which many raids against western Pennsylvania had been launched.

Fourth and finally, there was an odd proposal to emigrate across the Ohio and form a new state circulating among frontier communities. Handbills had even been posted in Wheeling proposing that future emigrants rendezvous at Wheeling on May 20 to begin their movement west.[38] Irvine believed that a significant portion of people who warmed to the idea simply wanted land, but he also suspected the proposal was a British plot to separate frontier residents from their American citizenship and bring them over to the British side in the war. Indeed, the Americans could not defend their border along the Ohio, much less on the other side. So emigrants could only hope for Indian restraint and British promises for their security. The general warned Washington, "Should these people actually emigrate, they must be either entirely cut off, or immediately take protection from the British."[39] In truth, illegal emigration had been a problem for some time and ran counter to US policy during the war. Colonel Brodhead had been forced to deal with it and enlist state militia support in evicting such squatters.[40] In that light, it is possible to view the Sandusky campaign as a precursor to acquiring land across the Ohio. By endorsing a military campaign to the Sandusky, Irvine might preempt a mass emigration on May 20, as William Moore suggested in his correspondence with the general.[41] Irvine had to wrestle with all these motivations among various individuals and factions on the frontier.

IRVINE GAVE CONSIDERABLE THOUGHT to a campaign across Ohio while planning an attack on Detroit, collecting intelligence, planning routes, and contemplating alternatives. Even though the proposed Sandusky campaign differed significantly from his preferred aim, much of the work remained relevant. He still believed "If we act offensively it will draw the whole attention of the enemy to their own defense, by which our settlements will have peace; and such of the militia as do not go on the expedition will have time to raise crops."[42] Although he was writing about Detroit, his observation still applied to a spoiling attack on the Sandusky.

Despite the failure of Captain Springer's April scouting mission across the Ohio, Irvine estimated there were some three hundred regulars at Detroit and seven hundred to one thousand more Canadian militia. Moreover, he believed the British were mobilizing roughly thirteen Indian nations in the area, with elements of the Shawnee and Ottawa moving closer to Detroit, and thus the Sandusky, and that five nations had already moved to the Sandusky to be closer to British supply depots at Detroit. All told, he concluded the British could assemble another one thousand Indians at Detroit within ten days' notice.[43] In short, Irvine's own information raised the possibility that a campaign to the Sandusky would mean running considerable risks, quite possibly marching into a hornet's nest of British, Canadian, and Indian adversaries. The general concluded that an offensive had to move quickly, before the British could mobilize all these resources to oppose it.

Ohio was wet and boggy, slowing the passage of men and horses. Irvine thought the opportune time to march on Detroit was early August, when "the waters are low; morasses and soft, rich meadows dried up."[44] An overland offensive over dry ground could advance more quickly and hope to achieve some measure of surprise. Although the offensive morphed from an assault on Detroit to a raid on Sandusky, speed remained paramount in Irvine's mind. As men responded to the April recruiting posters and began to assemble, Irvine predicted "their march will be so rapid they will probably in a great degree effect a surprise."[45]

So when he finally assented to the campaign, giving it an official imprimatur, Irvine took all these things into account: the varying motivations of those volunteering for the campaign, the different interests of those who had proposed it, political conditions in the territory, command jealousies among the counties from which volunteers came, the ability of the British and Indians to respond, the need to advance swiftly, fallout from the Gnadenhutten massacre, and the desire to avoid a repeat.

LOCAL LEADERS WANTED IRVINE to command the expedition, even though he could provide nothing substantive in the way of Continental manpower or resources. He considered it and was tempted but declined, believing it was inconsistent with the spirit of Washington's orders.[46] Instead, he crafted a set of instructions addressed to the commander, who was yet to be determined. He dated them May 14, six days before the designated rendezvous of volunteers at Mingo Bottom on the Ohio River.

The general stressed the military nature and purpose of the expedition, "to destroy with fire and sword (if practicable) the Indian town and settlements at Sandusky, by which we hope to give ease and safety to inhabitants of this country." He emphasized the importance of achieving this military goal repeatedly. To that end, he offered some operational advice: "Your best chance for success will be, if possible, to effect a surprise; and though this will be difficult, yet, by forced and rapid marches, it may, in a great degree, be accomplished."[47] Moreover, he recommended a dawn attack, which necessitated maintaining some distance before a rapid, long march the day and night before.

Next, Irvine tackled the issue of command and rank. "It will be highly expedient that all matters respecting rank or command should be well determined and clearly understood. . . . This precaution, in case of accident or misfortune, may be of great importance."[48] As it already stood, Pennsylvania's militia had a convoluted system of rank and seniority. While county lieutenants and sublieutenants held the rank of colonel and lieutenant colonel, it was still necessary to rank them and delineate seniority within the state. The militia law provided for a system that laid out seniority from county to county, not from officer to officer, radiating by county outward from Philadelphia. Thus, colonels closer to Philadelphia held seniority over colonels farther away.[49] (Lower ranking officers in the militia also rotated through classes in permanent billets and then were reassigned to active billets as classes were called up.) Since the Sandusky campaign was to be conducted as a volunteer campaign rather than through a call-up of the militia, the relevance of the entire system was suspect, or at least poised to become a bone of contention. Thus, Irvine strongly urged the commanding officer to work through the entire issue with his men, and any volunteering militia officers, before the expedition departed Mingo Bottom.

The vague and ad hoc nature of a such a large volunteer expedition raised other questions, particularly about discipline. The near mutiny of called-up militia and subsequent murder of prisoners during Brodhead's 1781 campaign against the Delaware, the Gnadenhutten massacre, and the subsequent attack on Killbuck's Island made clear the all-too-real tendency of the locals to act as they chose. In a military campaign, such indiscipline could not only be risky but downright dangerous. With that in mind, Irvine argued that the volunteers should consider themselves as militia, subject to the militia law and regulations, which contained rules regarding discipline. He pointed out that the decision to count the campaign against required militia service made the militia law and regulations applicable. It was an artful construction, since the campaign was undertaken outside the rules of a militia call-up. Colonels Cook of Westmoreland County and

Marshel of Washington County could have tried to call up the militia for the operation, although it was outside the county borders, and imposed the laws and regulations regarding behavior. But they chose not to. For his part, the Continental general had no authority to impose such rules, despite his attempt to argue they obtained.[50]

In the next figurative breath, Irvine moved on to something that must have been on his mind: preventing a repeat of the Gnadenhutten massacre. He could not be explicit about it, however, as the massacre was still popular in some quarters and a portion of the expected volunteers had undoubtedly participated. First, he flattered his audience, describing the volunteers as "virtuous and disinterested a set of men as you will have the honor to command." To the modern ear familiar with the massacre, it might sound like high sarcasm, but Irvine hoped to achieve a real purpose, and chastising his audience would not help. "It will be incumbent on you especially who will have the command, and on every individual, to act, in every instance in such a manner as will reflect honor on, and add reputation to, the American arms—always having in view the law of arms, of nations, or independent states."[51] The law of arms, nations, or independent states was unrecognizable on the frontier, and it is not likely that many of the volunteers had the first notion of what constraints or practices that reference was meant to affirm. Of course, it generally precluded the mass slaughter of unarmed and unresisting people.

Second, Irvine raised the issue of prisoners. "Should any prisoners, British, or in the service or pay of Britain or their allies, fall into your hands—if it should prove inconvenient for you to bring them off, you will, nevertheless, take special care to liberate them on parole, in such a manner as to insure liberty for an equal number of our people in their hands."[52] Summary execution was not an option. Given the frequency with which prisoners taken by either Indians or Americans on the frontier war were killed, it is tempting to view this instruction as a preemptive attempt to avoid blame if things went badly, as one might reasonably expect them to, given recent events. Such a cynical interpretation is unjust to Brigadier General Irvine. For much of the war, Continental civil and military authorities at Pittsburgh sought to preserve some measure of peace and humanity on the frontier. Early on, they even had Indian allies in the process. Of course, circumstances changed, and the ongoing war led to escalating violence. Nevertheless, even in fall 1781, Continental military officers had tried to protect peaceful Native Americans from undifferentiated revenge attacks by whites living on the frontier. That they had failed does not erase the sincerity of their intentions. In this case, Irvine's highlighting of the value of prisoners right after mentioning the importance of following international law and arguing that the rules of discipline applied suggest he was trying to avoid a repeat of the recent past. As we will see, he took additional steps in that direction as the campaign was organized.

Irvine's tenuous leverage over the organization, purpose, command, and conduct of the campaign was limited to (1) his approval, which gave the campaign a patina of respectability, (2) his local political influence, which was limited but real given his authority at Fort Pitt, (3) the amount of respect he commanded due to his military experience and rank, and (4) any material support he could offer to the campaign. If pushed too far, the local community could decide at any point that Irvine's leverage meant little, so he had to be careful how he used it.

On the question of material support, he had next to nothing to offer but a small amount of powder and some flints. He was forced to inform local leaders that volunteers must provide their own horses, shot, powder, and food for thirty days.[53] Volunteers would replace any horses lost on the expedition and keep any property they could claim as having been their own from the plunder seized.[54] However, he did send two Continental officers with the volunteers: Lieutenant John Rose, who was Irvine's aide-de-camp and Dr. John Knight, who had served in the 19th and 9th Virginia Regiments and was now surgeon of the 7th Virginia posted at Fort Pitt under Colonel Gibson. Both had extensive experience with large bodies of soldiers and offered skills that western militia officers sometimes lacked. They will figure prominently in what follows. Finally, Irvine used his local influence and respect to shape the vote for the volunteer campaign's commanding officer.

This being a volunteer expedition, participants would elect their own officers rather than following the existing militia command structure. Lieutenant Colonel David Williamson was the logical choice to command. He was popular, led the expedition to Gnadenhutten that preceded the Sandusky campaign, proposed the Sandusky campaign, provided some of the supplies for it, and already held a military rank in the Washington County militia, from which most of the volunteers would come. Instead, the Continental general preferred Colonel William Crawford and cryptically reported to Washington that he had "taken some pains to get Colonel Crawford appointed to command."[55] With that, Irvine's leverage over the affair was exhausted.

WILLIAM CRAWFORD WAS WELL KNOWN to Washington. They were both Virginians who served on Braddock's march to seize the Forks of the Ohio at the beginning of the French and Indian War and survived the Battle of Monongahela. Later, when Washington commanded Virginia's forces, Crawford was commissioned as an ensign in Virginia's service, primarily scouting the frontier and garrisoning frontier forts. By 1758, he had joined the Virginia troops marching with Washington on Forbes's campaign, which finally captured Fort Duquesne at the Forks of the Ohio in November 1758. While Washington eventually retired from Virginia's service and settled in at Mt. Vernon, Crawford stayed on the frontier, becoming a lieutenant and eventually a captain.

During this time, Crawford traveled all over today's southwest Pennsylvania, which Virginia claimed. Like many of his generation, the war veteran decided his future lay in the West, where land was cheaper. In 1766, at age forty-four, he moved his wife, Hannah, and their family over the Appalachians and settled along the Youghiogheny River, optimistically naming the small cabin he built Spring Garden.[56] It was just off Braddock's road and became a regular stop for travelers moving back and forth from Pittsburgh.

George Washington and William Crawford soon went into the land-speculation business together. The future president wanted to acquire valuable land along the Ohio River and its major tributaries.[57] Crawford would act as the surveyor, agent, and partner. Washington would raise the capital, take the business risks, and provide some political muscle. Crawford would provide the labor.

Crawford and his brother, Valentine, became frequent visitors to Mt. Vernon, and in 1770, Washington joined them on the Youghiogheny for an autumn trip to and down the Ohio River to visit their land acquisitions. He was satisfied with Crawford's work and later commended Crawford to George Croghan, a land speculator in Pennsylvania and an Indian agent at Fort Pitt. As Virginia and Pennsylvania tussled over land titles and boundaries, it was important to secure rights and ownership recognized by both colonies. Washington had helped Crawford secure a role in Virginia to their mutual benefit. Now he wanted to secure a similar place for Crawford with Pennsylvania as the two colonies sought to survey their borders. He wrote Croghan:

> I presume there will be Surveyors appointed to different Districts, in order that the Land may be run out as fast as possible; in that case I wou'd beg leave to recommend Captn Crawford to your friendly notice as a person who would be glad to be employed, and as one who I dare say wou'd discharge the duty with honesty & care—thro' your means he might come in for a share of this business—I am persuaded also, that he would not be wanting in gratitude for the favor.[58]

As if to demonstrate the veracity of Washington's words, Crawford and his extended family, which had begun arriving in the Youghiogheny River Valley, spent years moving up and down the Ohio making some improvements on the acreage he and Washington had surveyed, solidifying their land claims.

As complex as competing colonial border claims could be, uncertainty about political borders also created opportunities for settlers in Virginia and Pennsylvania. Both colonies could offer rewards, such as title recognition or public office, to influential locals in an effort to buy their loyalty. Despite his close ties to Virginia, Crawford was appointed justice of the peace for Cumberland County, Pennsylvania. When Bedford County was carved out of Cumberland County in 1771, Crawford became a justice of the peace in that county as well. The same thing happened in 1773, when Pennsylvania created Westmoreland County out of Bedford County.[59] Consequently, he had a stake in Pennsylvania's regional claims.

That same year, the dual colonial loyalties that occasionally signaled opportunity for a creative local with connections began to reveal one of the downsides of success: the need to choose one side in the conflict and risk alienating the other. Crawford became surveyor for the Ohio Company. One of its largest investors was John Murray, Earl of Dunmore, the new governor of Virginia. Lord Dunmore paid a visit to Spring Garden in 1773 to gauge the status of his investments. Crawford happily updated him on completed surveys, while Dunmore promised to confirm patents for the lands Crawford personally claimed. It was good news, as long as his Pennsylvania neighbors did not object. But Crawford's private interests in the business successes of leading Virginians may have conflicted with his public responsibilities as a justice of the peace in Pennsylvania.[60]

Britain began withdrawing its military forces from Pittsburgh in 1772 and created a power vacuum. After his 1773 visit, Dunmore decided to fill it. At the beginning of 1774, Dr. John Connolly rode into Pittsburgh as an agent of Virginia, asserted the colony's sovereignty over the area, occupied the abandoned Fort Pitt, and called out the local militia under Virginia's authority. He announced that the jurisdiction of Westmoreland County, Pennsylvania, did not reach all the way to the Forks of the Ohio, essentially curtailing William Crawford's authority as a justice of the peace. Then Connolly began creating a parallel government structure. The conflict between Virginia and Pennsylvania escalated as authorities in Philadelphia took their own countermeasures.

The extended Crawford clan took advantage of the situation. William Crawford's half-brother, John Stephenson, and his son-in-law, William Harrison, took the oath as Connolly's subalterns in the new local Virginia militia. Crawford concluded it would solidify the land claims he and Washington were making along the Ohio River and its tributaries and informed his business partner.[61] At the same time, he fulfilled his responsibilities to Pennsylvania by reporting on events to its governor, John Penn.[62] It was a delicate balancing act but not unprecedented on the weakly governed frontier.

Against this backdrop, cross-border raids between white settlers and Indian raiding parties escalated. By spring, Dunmore and Virginia mobilized their resources to go to war against the Shawnee. William Crawford offered to recruit soldiers and would lead a contingent from the area. Despite his official post as a Pennsylvanian, Crawford went to war as a Virginian.[63] While Britain's Indian Department worked to isolate the Shawnee diplomatically, Virginia mobilized, and Dunmore made his way across the colony to lead the campaign in person. Militia from the frontier counties focused on scouting and building forts as places of refuge and supply depots. Crawford, still a captain in the Virginia militia, led a contingent to the junction of Wheeling Creek and the Ohio River, where they built Fort Fincastle.[64] Although several units operated out of Fort Fincastle, Crawford led the largest group of some two hundred to three hundred militiamen. Over the summer, Crawford was promoted to major, and his command grew to roughly five hundred men. Dunmore ordered Crawford and his men to build another depot and fort at the mouth of the Hockhocking River, which became Fort Gower.[65] When Dunmore finally crossed the Ohio at Fort Gower in October, Crawford's division became the vanguard of Dunmore's right wing.[66] It was an army of over 1,100 men.

Dunmore's left wing was to advance down the Kanawha River before uniting with the right closer to the Shawnee towns. The Shawnee, caught in a pincer, engaged Dunmore's left wing at Point Pleasant, where the Kanawha and Ohio Rivers meet. After

a close-fought battle, the Shawnee and a few of their allied tribes
withdrew. Both of Dunmore's columns advanced into the Ohio
country. The Shawnee eventually sued for peace, and Dunmore
engaged in a round of diplomacy with them at a place he dubbed
Camp Charlotte. While there, the Virginians learned that a group
of recalcitrant Mingo Indians up the Scioto River planned to with-
draw to Lake Erie with their prisoners. Dunmore selected Crawford to lead a quick march of roughly 240 militiamen against the
Mingo village at the fork of the Scioto. In a quick fight, Crawford's
men killed six elderly warriors, wounded a few more people, and
captured fourteen others.[67] It was his only notable combat during
Dunmore's War, but William Crawford had learned quite a bit
about mobilizing, organizing, and leading large and diverse
groups of amateur soldiers.[68]

WHY REVIEW THIS PORTION of Crawford's life, which predated the
Sandusky campaign by decades? Simply, the vote to command the
Sandusky expedition was going to be close and contentious. Crawford had thrown his lot in with Virginia during the struggle for
control of the area, but a growing share of the region's settlers
identified as Pennsylvanians. After the Battles of Lexington and
Concord in 1775, political authorities in the east generally put
off resolving the conflicting state claims and allegiances. This
caused problems when it came time to coordinate the frontier's
defense. Indeed, as we have seen, some defended the frontier
counties as called-up Pennsylvania militia while Virginia's local
military leaders still had to await orders from the east. That was
part of the reason Virginia's response to Irvine's military conference in April had been so disappointing. It would be unnatural
for volunteers accustomed to Pennsylvanians as their local military leaders to suddenly reverse course and defer to a quasi Virginian who had spent much of the war fighting in the east. To
complicate matters further, Crawford was sixty years old. Early biographies and stories about the campaign dated his birth in 1732,

but they were accepting and repeating errors made in the first documented account of his death. Subsequent historians relied on it and perpetuated the error. Allen W. Scholl conducted the most comprehensive genealogical study of the Crawford family and concluded William Crawford was born in 1722, although an exact date remained uncertain. The most modern biography of Crawford accepts Scholl's work.[69] His best days in the field were behind him. A campaign deep into enemy territory might prove just too much.

That said, Crawford had much to offer in commanding a volunteer campaign. Save those serving with the Continental Army at Fort Pitt, Crawford may have been the most experienced field-grade officer in the area. While Crawford was fortifying the Ohio frontier and advancing into Indian territory during Dunmore's War, eastern elites were gathering at the First Continental Congress. Everything changed after Lexington and Concord, albeit more slowly than we often recognize in the twenty-first century. On February 13, 1776, Virginia commissioned William Crawford as a lieutenant colonel and second in command of the 5th Virginia Regiment. He left the regiment that summer when it marched north to join Washington's army outside New York; he had been promoted to colonel and appointed to command the 7th Virginia, still in Williamsburg.[70] By November, he had been transferred yet again to command the 13th Virginia, most of which had been raised around Fort Pitt.

Crawford and his new levies finally joined Washington's main army in August 1777, just in time for the Philadelphia Campaign. At Brandywine, his regiment was posted at Chadd's Ford as part of Nathanael Greene's division and saw fighting near the end of the battle.[71] Then, at Germantown, still under Greene, the men broke when the Virginia Brigade became disordered in the mist. Within the month, Washington directed the colonel to return to Pittsburgh and form a new brigade of Virginia militia.[72] Once there, Crawford "advised" the Western Department commander, Brigadier General Edward Hand, during the latter's attempt to raid a British supply depot on the Cuyahoga River, a fiasco known

derisively as "The Squaw Campaign" because it resulted in the unnecessary deaths of friendly Delaware Indians in 1778. At the end
of the year, Crawford again marched into the Ohio country, this
time under the command of Brigadier General Lachlan McIntosh, Hand's replacement. McIntosh was bound for Detroit and
built Fort McIntosh on the Beaver River and Fort Laurens on the
Muskingum before returning to Pittsburgh. He intended to return in spring 1779 and continue to Detroit, but McIntosh was
relieved first and replaced with Colonel Daniel Brodhead. Directed to support an offensive up the Allegheny River in 1779,
Brodhead abandoned Fort Laurens to use its garrison on his
march north.[73] Crawford joined Brodhead on this latest advance
from Fort Pitt as well.

Along the way, Crawford continued to receive state appoint-
ments from Virginia or its counties.[74] But his star in the army had
faded. His position in the Continental Line was unresolved, and
he was on his own to address it.[75] By 1781, his health was failing.
He wanted to join George Rogers Clark on a campaign against
the Shawnee on the Scioto River "if my health will permit; but I
am very unhealthy lately, having got much cold on the two last
expeditions," he wrote to Washington.[76] Nevertheless, with Irvine
declining the command of an advance to the Sandusky, no one
else in the area had as much experience leading men on the battlefield or on the frontier. Though he might think of himself, and
be thought of, as a Virginian, Crawford could plausibly hope to
win a vote among the Pennsylvanians, as well as the Virginians
who volunteered for the expedition.

GENERAL IRVINE MET WITH Colonel Crawford at Pittsburgh before the latter set out for the scheduled rendezvous at Mingo Bottom. Crawford arrived at Pittsburgh on May 18, then set out for
Mingo Bottom on May 20.[77] As the general related, Crawford
thought they would need four hundred men to reach the Sandusky and engage the Indians. He feared going with fewer.[78]

Crawford requested that Irvine's adjutant Lieutenant Rose and Dr. Knight of the 7th Virginia accompany the expedition.[79]

Various groups of volunteers had departed their homes for Mingo Bottom as early as May 15. It took time to travel over primitive roads, trails, and old game paths, ensuring that many men had been on the road for days before the rendezvous at Mingo Bottom.[80] Crawford encountered about one hundred men from Westmoreland County at the home of John Canon on May 20 and finally arrived at the rendezvous on May 21 with Lieutenant Rose.[81] Knight was not far behind. News, including travel schedules, spread unevenly on the frontier. So despite the intended May 20 rendezvous, delays, including that necessitated by Crawford's extended visit to Pittsburgh, were inevitable. Well after May 20, lines of mounted frontier farmers, traders, merchants, and hunters continued streaming all across southwestern Pennsylvania and northwestern Virginia bound for the rendezvous at Mingo Bottom. Crawford originally hoped to cross the Ohio on Wednesday, May 22, but the expedition waited two more days.

Two additional factors for delaying after Crawford's arrival have to be considered. First, volunteers continued to arrive at the east bank rally for days after the scheduled rendezvous. Crawford wanted as many volunteers as possible in his expedition, and waiting stood in his favor. Second, there was an election to hold, which Crawford was supposed to win. He may well have needed the time to conduct a little campaigning. The volunteers were intensely divided on the matter of command, with Crawford and Williamson each having similar numbers of supporters. Crawford might be more experienced, but Williamson had stayed on the frontier and led two campaigns to the Muskingum, including the tragic attack on Gnadenhutten just over two months earlier, while Crawford fought in the east. Despite its horror, the massacre at Gnadenhutten was still popular in some quarters. Moreover, Williamson had agitated for the campaign to Sandusky and provided some portion of the supplies.

Tensions were high enough that Lieutenant Rose reported the whole affair might fall apart. Indeed, his own presence caused some "uneasiness" that he might take command until he declared at an officer's meeting that he had no such intentions and was only expected to act as an aide-de-camp to the commanding officer. Only on May 24, after the vote, three days after Crawford's arrival and two days after Crawford's intended crossing date, could Rose report, "My fears that the present expedition would miscarry have been dispelled this very moment only. Colonels Williamson and Crawford did seem to have numerous and obstinate adherents."[82] In the end, Crawford won by only 5 votes out of 465 cast.[83]

The wild card in the election was Colonel Marshel, the lieutenant of Washington County and Williamson's militia superior. Marshel was present at Mingo Bottom but did not accompany the expedition. Technically, because it was a volunteer campaign, he had to rely on influence rather than formal authority to affect outcomes. The two-months credit against militia service for volunteers was largely his carrot to dangle. It involves a bit of guesswork, but it would not be difficult to conclude that the "pains to get Colonel Crawford appointed to command" that Irvine took involved some sort of side deal with Marshel. Indeed, in early May, Marshel admitted to Irvine that he had issued military supplies from Washington County to support the Sandusky expedition as a priority and that he expected Irvine to make up the difference for the militia called up to protect the frontier per the April strategy meeting.[84] A little bit of horse trading to swing an election would not be unprecedented, although it is speculation.

If there were hard feelings, they were quickly papered over. Marshel reported to Irvine, "A perfect harmony subsisted among officers and men, and all were in high spirits."[85] To his credit, Williamson rose to the occasion after the vote and endorsed Crawford as the new commander. Rose reported to Irvine, "I cannot but give Colonel Williamson the utmost credit for his exhorting the whole to be unanimous after the election had been made known, and cheerfully submitted to be second in command. I think if it had been otherwise, Crawford would have pushed home and very likely we should have dispersed; which would have been likewise the case if Williamson had not behaved with so much prudence."[86]

With the issue of overall command decided, the volunteers still needed to choose the officers who would lead them. Colonel Thomas Gattis became the third in command, Lieutenant Colonel John McLelland fourth, and Major James Brenton fifth. Daniel Leet became the brigade major, and both Knight and Rose were confirmed in their roles as surgeon and aide.[87] After the morning election, Crawford and his officers began organizing their command. The volunteers divided into eighteen companies averaging twenty-seven men per company, though they were in fact unevenly distributed and likely wanted to remain in their self-determined groups of friends and neighbors. The total eventually came to 488 volunteers, including those who continued to trickle in after the election was over. The vast majority, perhaps 350, came from Washington County. Twenty or so hailed from Ohio County, Virginia, and the balance were from Westmoreland County, Pennsylvania.[88] Unfortunately, some of the volunteers had been called up for militia service and failed to turn out for frontier defense, leaving at least one militia officer pleading poverty to Irvine when it came to meeting the goals of the April strategy conference.[89]

Crawford and his officers segmented the volunteers into five main groups arranged in four columns. First came the advance guard of one company, followed by the advance body of four companies. The main body held four of the larger companies followed by a rear body comprising the four smallest companies. Then there was a rear guard of one company. Scouts and spies would move ahead of the small army while "ambush men" would remain at the rear keeping an eye out for any enemies seeking to maneuver into ambush positions. Crawford nominally assigned flankers on either side for the same purpose.[90]

Much would depend on the scouts, John Slover, Jonathan Zane, and Thomas Nichols, who were to be paid the extraordinary sum of nine pounds each.[91] Although Crawford had considerable experience in the Ohio country, much of it was farther south, along rivers and streams that fed into the Ohio River. The Sandusky drained in a northerly direction into Lake Erie. The Native American nations there, particularly the Wyandot, had allied with the British in 1777. Few Americans had been there since. Slover, Zane, and Nichols might have more familiarity with the region, but by 1782 their knowledge was outdated.

Williamson was to command from the lead. Lieutenant Rose described him as "brave as Caesar and active: but divested of conduct. Fond of thrusting himself into danger, he leaves everything else to chance—He has some obscure notions of military matters . . . but is quite ignorant how to dispose of men or how to fight them to advantage." Aware of Williamson's political popularity and "man of the people" persona when interacting with his men, Rose thought the second in command guilty of putting on airs and condescending to let "Bigotted notions stand him in lieu of arguments." That said, Rose also found him open to advice and possessing some latent talent. [92]

In the main body, Lieutenant Colonel McLelland would lead the right wing and Major Brenton the left. Rose had little to say about McLelland, who hailed from Westmoreland County. He commanded the fourth battalion of the county's militia and would have worked with many of the volunteers in the past.[93] Rose considered Brenton "Our Best Field Officer. He has imbibed very good notions of military matters, founded upon by praxise in Indian Wars. He is schemy in an engagement—Quite brave enough, to lead his men into action—and not wanting of resources to extricate himself out of danger, and discern it before hand."[94] Gattis commanded the rear body. He was a field officer with the Westmoreland County militia. Rose considered him at least competent. "G. is like the greatest part of Mankind, not possessed of any extraordinary qualifications—But withall, a good Officer Attentive to regularity on a march, and not wanting of personal bravery—Performs his duty with chearfullness, and obeys Orders without murmuring."[95]

Daniel Leet was a resident of Washington County but had been a frontier surveyor for Virginia before the war. He served with the

13th Virginia as quartermaster and paymaster and was at Valley Forge. In 1778, he accompanied Brigadier General McIntosh as an adjutant during the march to construct Fort Laurens and then became a sublieutenant to Colonel Marshel of Washington County in 1781. Like Crawford, he also held political positions as a land commissioner and justice of the peace for Washington County, but his involvement in militia activity was on the decline. He resigned his militia position as a sublieutenant of the county just before the volunteer expedition set out.[96] Rose remarked that Leet was "too easy and neglectfull for his post, though the only man, any ways acquainted with duty. He is allowed to have behaved with much Bravery; yet, I believe, unnecessarily so."[97]

WHAT EXACTLY QUALIFIED JOHN ROSE, a mere lieutenant, to offer such lofty pronouncements about the character and performance of the command structure? He was, in truth, one of the most interesting characters on the Pennsylvania frontier. "John Rose" was an assumed name. Irvine's adjutant and Crawford's aide-de-camp was in fact Baron Gustavus de Rosenthal, a Russian from an area along the Baltic Sea known as Livonia, but today divided between the countries of Estonia and Latvia. While on the palace grounds in St. Petersburg, the Russian capital, Rosenthal took offense when another nobleman slapped his uncle. A duel followed. Rosenthal killed the offender then fled to England. Afterward, he briefly served as a surgeon in the Royal Navy. When the colonies rebelled, Rosenthal decided to join the Americans and turned up at Valley Forge, calling himself John Rose. Naturally, Rosenthal, who would not identify himself or his background, sought a commission. None were available, but he impressed enough people to secure an appointment as a surgeon's mate in a hospital. While at Valley Forge, Rose crossed paths with Irvine, newly exchanged after his capture during the Canadian campaign. Irvine had been a surgeon in the Royal Navy and soon recognized that the Russian's skills were subpar. Yet Irvine also saw bravery and intelligence in Rose and had him transferred to his own brigade, eventually gaining an appointment for him as a lieutenant in the Pennsylvania Line. Inevitably, the preferential treatment for a foreigner caused jealousies. Rosenthal left his regiment to join the Continental Navy in 1780, going to sea as a surgeon, only to be captured and imprisoned in New York. He was exchanged in 1781 and rejoined Irvine as an aide with the rank of major.[98] (That was how his rank was popularly understood during the Crawford campaign, but Irvine continued to refer to him as a lieutenant in his official correspondence with Washington.)

TWO

The Advance

DEEP IN THE OHIO COUNTRY, Native Americans and the British knew the volunteers were coming. They had known it for months, perhaps before Crawford. In April, while Brigadier General Irvine was contemplating the requests for support of a volunteer campaign and recruiting handbills were circulating, the Indians continued their raids along the frontier, killing settlers, taking others prisoner, burning farms, and seizing livestock. On April 8, Simon Girty, a British Indian agent, sent a note to the commander at Detroit, Major Arent Schuyler DePeyster, informing him that a prisoner taken in those raids revealed that a campaign to the Sandusky was in the offing.[1] Confirmation from Girty's boss, Alexander McKee, arrived in Detroit a few days later.[2] Shortly afterward, DePeyster learned that Lord Charles Cornwallis had surrendered his army at Yorktown roughly six months earlier. To complicate matters, he received the news from his Indian agents, not his superiors in Quebec. So the Indians knew it as well. It was not clear what that meant for Detroit—whether the Americans would turn their forces westward to the frontier or remain focused on the east—but DePeyster had to prepare for an imminent attack just the same. He requested reinforcements.

Fortuitously for DePeyster, when Brigadier General Henry Powell at Fort Niagara heard of the impending American offensive, he took the initiative and dispatched twenty-four rangers under the command of Lieutenant John Turney to Detroit on May 10. They were originally scheduled to replace a ranger unit already there, but Powell opted to leave those men in Detroit as well.[3] In short, the British were sending more men to counter the volunteers headed for Sandusky before the volunteers assembled at Mingo Bottom.

DePeyster was not sure how word of Yorktown would affect his Native American allies. If they concluded that the British were going to lose the war, the less belligerent tribes might seek a separate peace with the Americans, using what leverage they had before it was gone. Worse, they might simply switch sides, for which there was ample precedent on the frontier. He was particularly concerned about the Wyandot.[4] So he called a council at Detroit on May 15 to remind the Lake Indians of past successes, emphasize the value of their mutual interests, and renew his own commitment to their joint cause of making war on the Americans.

On the British side, deputy Indian agent Alexander McKee, Captain William Caldwell from the Corps of Rangers, a Lieutenant Brooks of the British 8th Regiment, and some interpreters accompanied the major. The Indians were represented by chiefs and warriors from the Wyandot, Ottawa, Chippewa/Ojibwe, and Potawatomi nations, the hardened core of the Native American members of the British coalition in the West, as well as representatives from more distant tribes.[5] DePeyster presented two war belts. A larger one from the Iroquois Confederation reminded the western nations of their commitment to the war. A smaller one had been created by the western nations and presented to the Shawnee, Delaware, and Mingo as a pledge of future support. Its presentation signified a call by those Indians for the western nations to make good on their promise. DePeyster also offered smaller wampum strings as a reminder that he had honored requests for army and ammunition in the past. In short, the western Native American nations owed the Iroquois, the threatened tribes, and the British.

Next, the major raised the issue of early spring raids. Several western tribes had petitioned him to support such raids just a few months earlier, but he had held them back, believing "it was better to detain you until we heard of the Enemy's coming into the Indian Country that you might then be ready to meet them in a great body and repulse them."[6] Such restraint, of course, would have been news to frontier settlers in Pennsylvania and Virginia, who believed that attacks had intensified early in 1782 due to a round of favorable weather, but it was DePeyster's way of heightening the sense of drama.

Then DePeyster made his big announcement: "The day before yesterday I had an express from the Chiefs of St. Dooskey who inform me that they were out against the Enemy and saw them in number pass the Ohio opposite to Wheelin—a Deserter from the Enemy is now at St. Dooskey who reports that their design is for St. Dooskey."[7] The specific intelligence was premature and inaccurate, but the news served its purpose since word of the impending volunteer campaign had already spread. DePeyster announced that at the request of the Shawnee, Delaware, and Mingo he would no longer provide alcohol to the gathered tribes, a sign of the seriousness with which he took the threat. But he promised to let the liquor flow after the Americans were repulsed. Several Indian leaders complained about the taps closing, but after a Huron chief pledged to sharpen his hatchet and fight, other Indian leaders joined in a war chant and DePeyster reopened the taps while everyone prepared.[8] Because the American campaign was not aimed at Detroit, what really mattered was the state of the Indian nations along the Sandusky and any reinforcements DePeyster could send there. Of course, he did not know that with certainty in May. So reassurances that the closest tribes continued to embrace the British as allies and would take up the war hatchet could only make him more secure in Detroit and, ultimately, more willing to dispatch his own limited resources to the Sandusky.

DePeyster ordered Captain William Caldwell to depart for Sandusky with two small companies of rangers, his own and another posted at Detroit. As they boarded the sloop *Faith* the next day, Lieutenant Turney and his men arrived on the *Hope*. Together they totaled eighty-four officers and men. Speed was critical, so the British would rush forward aboard the sloops while their horses traveled overland around the western edge of Lake Erie. They may have had two small pieces of artillery.[9] The Great Lakes Indians whose aid DePeyster had secured in the council promised to follow as soon as they were ready.[10]

Caldwell and his men were from Butler's Rangers, a Loyalist unit organized in 1777. Colonel John Butler commanded them from Niagara, and they operated throughout the Great Lakes during the war, although most operations occurred in Pennsylvania and New York.[11] They routinely operated with Native Americans, particularly those led by Joseph Brant.[12] Caldwell and Turney were both early members; Caldwell's commission was dated December 24, 1777, and Turney's in February 1779.[13] The unit had been involved in campaigns in Pennsylvania's Wyoming and Cherry Valleys, both of which included Indian raids and involved the kind of excesses associated with frontier warfare. In 1778, the unit mustered six companies, moved into a group of barracks, and received the traditional green uniforms of ranger units. Normally they would be equipped with rifles, but a shortage of firearms on the frontier meant individual rangers often carried whatever weapons they brought or the British could supply from Niagara.[14] By 1782, Captain Caldwell was one of the most experienced leaders in the unit and had served at Detroit before. He was a suitable choice to lead British soldiers to the Sandusky, even if there were just eighty-four of them. Resisting the Americans would require much, much more.

While Caldwell and his rangers made their way by water, Captain Mathew Elliott accompanied a contingent of warriors from the tribes DePeyster had assembled on May 15. It was a paltry number between forty and fifty. By the time of the battle, Captain Caldwell noted just forty-four of the Lake Indians were in the fight.[15] British Indian agent Alexander McKee set out for the Upper Miami River basin, hoping to raise additional reinforcements from the Miami nation and any willing British allies in the area. It also fell to McKee to race to Shawnee territory, where he would convince that nation to dispatch warriors to support the Wyandot, Delaware, and Mingo on the Sandusky.[16]

BRITISH REACTIONS TO THE Sandusky campaign often received more attention than those of the Native Americans because they were better documented by British authorities often eager to portray themselves in command of events while simultaneously pleading for more resources and complaining about the fickleness and unreliability of their Indian allies. In truth, the clash between American volunteers advancing across the Ohio country and the tribes living along the Sandusky River, plus any allies they could gather, would determine the outcome of the campaign. The complaints of British officers notwithstanding, Native Americans fought the American Revolution in their own way for their own reasons, which did not always align with British practices or interests.

The largest Indian nation along the Sandusky was the Wyandot. At one time, the eastern Great Lakes were dominated by two large Native American groupings, the Iroquoian-speaking Haudenosaunee League along the southeastern shores of Lake Ontario and the Wendat, or Huron, Confederacy between Lake Ontario and Lake Huron.[17] Old-fashioned power politics and warfare occurred frequently between the two, and the Iroquois Confederacy eventually prevailed. As their confederacy broke up, some groupings of Wendat moved farther west, mixed with the Petun Indian nation, and eventually settled along Sandusky Bay as the Wyandot in the late 1730s.[18]

In 1747, the Wyandot in Ohio split over France's domination of the fur trade, with some opponents moving southeast to the confluence of the Muskingum and Walhonding Rivers. Others moved up the Sandusky River and established a village subsequently known as Upper Sandusky on the west side of the river. Several outlier village sites were also occupied at various times, and the population shifted from site to site. So the location of Upper Sandusky as a Wyandot village was conditional. This led to confusion on the part of the Americans, whose destination was Upper Sandusky but who did not know exactly where it was. Unfortunately, it also perplexed subsequent generations of historians.

The Wyandot had a reputation as fierce warriors and had fought the British in Pontiac's War. They sat out Dunmore's War and the early years of the American Revolution, but in 1777 answered Britain's call to take up the hatchet. Thereafter, Wyandot war parties were among the most aggressive frontier raiders in western Pennsylvania and Virginia. The dominant Wyandot leader was named Dunquat, Pomoacan to the Delaware, and Half King to whites. "Half King" was not a formal title, but, the Iroquois had a practice of sending some of their own trusted leaders as a kind of viceroy or regent to tribes they considered subordinate. Such people were sometimes known as half kings, and Dunquat hinted at some Iroquois lineage.[19] The connection may have been real; it may also have reflected white society trying to fit Dunquat and the Wyandot into an intellectual framework that whites already understood.

In August 1781, Dunquat led a large war party of some three hundred Wyandot, Delaware, Shawnee, Ottawa, and Chippewa warriors to the mission villages along the Muskingum River and stayed, over the objections of the Moravian missionaries and their Indian congregations.[20] He had two goals: remove the Christian Indians from the Muskingum, and establish a forward operating base from which to cross the Ohio River. They stayed nearly a month while Dunquat's warriors broke up into smaller groups and raided widely, striking homes, blockhouses, and farms in

Pennsylvania's Washington and Westmoreland Counties and northwestern Virginia, the very places from which the Sandusky campaign sprang in 1782. In September, Dunquat and his allies forcefully removed the Moravian Indians from their towns and relocated them to the Sandusky. It was not the first time Dunquat and the western Indians had used the Muskingum as a base from which to raid, but after the removal of their populations and the subsequent massacre and burning of the Muskingum villages by the Americans, it would prove to be the last.

The second-largest Indian nation along the upper Sandusky River was the Delaware. Known in their own language as the Lenape, whites had dubbed them Delaware after the river and bay on the East Coast named after Thomas West, Lord De Le Warr. It stuck. Never truly unified and scattered by internal division, war, defeat, famine, subordination to the Iroquois, and the spread of European immigrants, significant portions of the Delaware consolidated in eastern Ohio along the Muskingum River in the mid-eighteenth century.[21] They joined Pontiac's War but made peace in the face of a British offensive from Fort Pitt. Like the Wyandot, they largely stayed out of Dunmore's War and adopted a neutral posture in the first years of the American Revolution. Pressured by both sides to join the war, three Delaware leaders eventually signed the Treaty of Fort Pitt in 1778.[22] Ostensibly allying them with the Americans, the treaty exacerbated internal divisions. Wingenund and Hopocan, known as Captain Pipe among whites, led their more militant factions west to the Sandusky.[23] Of the remainder, a majority eventually joined the British in 1781, prompting Colonel Brodhead's campaign. After that, the remaining militant Delaware joined the rest of their nation on the Sandusky. A small, pro-American faction fled to Killbuck's Island near Pittsburgh, where settlers attacked them after the Gnadenhutten massacre.

The third group along the Sandusky was a scattering of Mingo Indians. The tribe had been formed largely by small groups of Seneca and Cayuga who migrated from their traditional Iroquois land and settled between Lake Erie and the Allegheny River, then moved farther downriver as time passed. Whether castoffs, refugees, or separatists, those leaving their Iroquois identities behind were called Mingwe by the Delaware, which morphed into Mingo among the English.[24] Lacking some of the cultural and political cohesion of other tribes, they often became scapegoats for whites and the Ohio Indians to blame when tensions escalated into violence. On the Sandusky, they were dispersed among the dominant Wyandot and Delaware villages, but they also provided warriors to defend the area.[25]

When faced with a white offensive toward their villages and surrounding fields, Native Americans often abandoned those villages and fled. It was usually the best way of protecting women and children who lived in the area. How the Sandusky Indians made their decision is lost to history, but sometime between the reports of an impending campaign and Crawford's arrival on the Sandusky plain, Dunquat and his fellow leaders opted to stay and meet the Americans as they approached. The exact number of warriors they could gather is unknown. Estimates have varied widely. Nineteenth century regional historians asserted some two hundred to five hundred Delaware and six hundred Wyandot warriors, including some from other tribes, waited for the Americans on the Sandusky.[26] More recent historians have lowered those numbers to some four hundred Wyandot and two hundred Delaware.[27] One of the campaign's prominent nineteenth century historians eventually gave up trying to estimate the number accurately and simply reported the Indians numbered "not less than two hundred."[28] Thus, we are left with a wide range of possible Indian combatants, from as high as thirteen hundred to as low as two hundred. Shawnee reinforcements, possibly numbering an additional 140 to 200 warriors, were on the way from the south, but Indian leaders on the Sandusky had no guarantee they would arrive in time.[29]

The tools we have to estimate the number of Indians gathered on the Sandusky are limited. We can safely discard the higher estimates of five hundred Delaware and six hundred Wyandot defenders plus up to two hundred Shawnee reinforcements. Even

General Irvine thought the British only capable of mustering one thousand Indians at Detroit given enough notice, and that figure included substantial numbers of the Great Lakes Indians to which Major DePeyster had already appealed, most of whom would not fight on the Sandusky. It is unlikely a larger number from two smaller tribes could assemble on the river. Even major offensives could not assemble this many Indians. DePeyster and the western Indians held a grand council to coordinate strategy for summer 1782 and opted to invade Kentucky and Virginia with two separate armies. The Kentucky-bound army comprised some six hundred warriors. The smaller, Virginia-bound force numbered some 250 to 350, plus 50 of Butler's Rangers under Captain Andrew Bradt.[30] Had the entirety of these forces assembled on the Sandusky, they would not reach the higher estimates of Indians available to Dunquat offered by some American historians.

It is tempting to split the difference and simply conclude that the Sandusky Indian warriors numbered somewhere between five hundred and six hundred, minus the Shawnee. While we cannot rule it out, a stronger case can be made that Dunquat and his allies had slightly fewer warriors available when they made the decision to face the advancing Americans. In August 1781, when Dunquat and his allies forcibly removed the Moravian Indians from the Muskingum, he brought a smaller force with him, including the militant Delaware led by Hopocan and Wingenund. John Heckewelder, a Moravian missionary who knew the Sandusky Indians well and spent several weeks observing them before being forced to leave his home, recorded that Dunquat brought roughly three hundred well-supplied warriors from the Wyandot, Delaware, Ottawa, Mohegan, and Shawnee nations.[31] After the Shawnee arrived, British Indian agent Alexander McKee reported that nearly five hundred Indians and rangers engaged the Americans, which lines up with the lower end of three hundred Wyandot, Delaware, and Mingo warriors after adding in the Shawnee and Lake Indian reinforcements.[32] In truth, the number of Indian warriors available for any single activity constantly fluctuated as war parties set out for, and returned from, the frontier. Still, if we

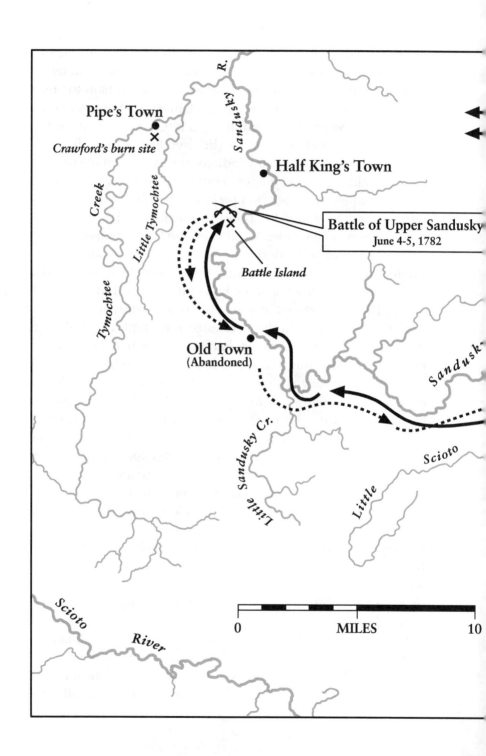

Pipe's Town

Crawford's burn site

Creek

Little Tymochtee

Tymochtee

Sandusky R.

Half King's Town

Battle of Upper Sandusky
June 4-5, 1782

Battle Island

Old Town
(Abandoned)

Little Sandusky Cr.

Sandusky

Scioto

Little

Scioto

River

0   MILES   10

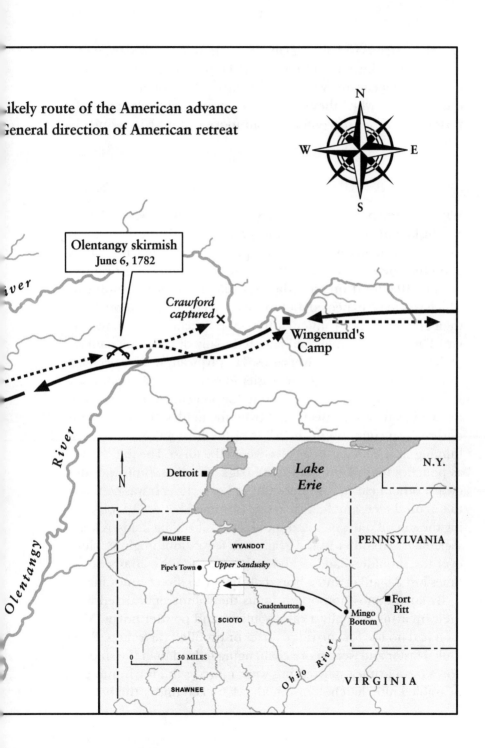

Likely route of the American advance
General direction of American retreat

N
W E
S

Olentangy skirmish
June 6, 1782

Crawford captured ✕

Wingenund's
Camp

River

River

Olentangy

N

Detroit ■

Lake Erie

N.Y.

MAUMEE
WYANDOT

Pipe's Town ● *Upper Sandusky*

PENNSYLVANIA

Gnadenhutten ●
SCIOTO

Mingo
Bottom

■ Fort
Pitt

Ohio River

0   50 MILES

SHAWNEE

VIRGINIA

take the warriors with which Dunquat removed the Moravian congregations as the core of his forces at Upper Sandusky, the Wyandot and Delaware who would face the Americans were
outnumbered when they decided to stay and fight, albeit with the
possibility of reinforcements from more distant tribes and the
British.

WHILE CAPTAIN CALDWELL'S RANGERS made their way to Upper
Sandusky and Dunquat's warriors prepared for battle, Crawford's
men shook themselves out of sleep, consumed their breakfasts,
gathered their horses, and finally set out from Mingo Bottom
around 10:00 AM on Saturday, May 25. They lacked uniforms,
which was to be expected, but there was a certain commonality in
their appearances. Frontier clothing was functional, even utilitar-
ian. Thus, frontiersmen had adopted many of the same patterns
of dress as their Indian adversaries. They typically wore moccasins,
which held up better and were easier to repair than shoes or boots
in the rough terrain. The same went for breeches or leggings, also
made of leather to protect limbs from the nettles, thorns, and underbrush so common in the wilds of the frontier. A large, loose
hunting shirt folded over a belt covered the torso. The folds served
as pouches that might hold small bags of bullets, flints, powder,
or any other gear it was important to keep close. It was common
to top off the ensemble with a wide-brimmed hat useful for keeping the sun off one's face and shoulders while tilling fields. A knapsack filled with other useful gear and a few rations might be slung
over the shoulder. Saddles and tack were primitive affairs, sometimes just a blanket and a horsehair halter to direct a mount.

By far the most important items the volunteers carried were
their firearms—usually a rifle—bullets, and powder horns. Most
men had no use for cartridge boxes or prefilled cartridges. Rifles
fouled faster and were more challenging to load than the smooth-
bores most armies sported but were more useful for hunting. A
wearable knife, hatchet, or tomahawk tucked under the belt was

a close second in importance, not only as a weapon but as a practical tool for butchering meat, cutting wood, and taking a life or scalp. Bayonets came from another world entirely. A canteen and larger knapsack often completed the kit. Over time, the image of a frontier settler, farmer, hunter, or scout took on an element of romance. C. W. Butterfield, an attorney and historian who lived close to Upper Sandusky, wrote the first campaign history in 1873 and described a stoic, even courageous and skilled marksman resigned to his duty to the community and focused entirely on the mission before him.[33]

Lieutenant Rose, who had spent years among Europe's upper crust, British naval officers, and American Continentals, had a decidedly less favorable opinion of the typical volunteer. Rather than choosing the best-suited horses, Rose observed, "he takes care to mount the very worst horse he has upon his farm . . . because the Owner expects to exchange him to advantage" with plundered animals.[34] Men carried extra rope with which to lead the horses they expected to seize.[35] Dr. Knight recalled "every one who had been plundered by the Indians, should, if the plunder could be found at their towns, have it again, proving it to be his property: and all horses lost on the expedition by unavoidable accident were to be replaced by horses taken in the enemy's country."[36] It was customary to take the balance of the remaining booty, sell it much in the way a privateer might, and divide the profits. Those eighty horses loaded with loot from Gnadenhutten might pale in comparison to the financial rewards volunteers could anticipate from a successful raid on the Wyandot towns.

Volunteers then overburdened their mounts with unnecessary provisions unmoored from the anticipated length of a campaign. The volunteer carried ample staples of bacon and flour, with an added allowance for whiskey. Rather than treating their horses as a critical component of military power, as proper cavalry or mounted infantry, volunteers simply viewed them as beasts of burden, to be ridden half to death. So, according to Rose, volunteers never dismounted to rest their horses or take turns breaking a trail.

Order and organization were also missing. When the volunteers departed Mingo Bottom that morning, they did not leave in the march order or formation Crawford had set, but in the order in which companies could be gotten ready. Williamson, who was supposed to be leading the advance guard, ended up at the rear.[37] After just ten miles of relatively easy riding through gentle slopes and an open wood, the column settled in around a good pasture, which they dubbed Camp Regulation. Rose, who rode with Williamson, came up on the army late in the day. He met briefly with Colonel Crawford, who assured him proper security measures were being taken. However, Rose "happened to take a circuit in the evening, & found to my great surprise, that several companies lay outside the picquets," while men grumbled about sentry duty after riding all day.[38]

Indeed, Rose generally looked down on the military skills of the volunteers. They should have been enrolled in the militia under the state's militia law and probably knew each other as neighbors and from past militia musters, but executing military maneuvers and conducting military operations as a body were not skills they possessed. Indeed, they could be quite dismissive when it came to basic martial practices. Keeping up a watch was critical to securing the force on its march, particularly when fighting Native Americans, who had a penchant for surprising lackadaisical adversaries. Finding sentries absent from their posts as he rode up to the force on the first day, Rose decided to participate in posting them himself. "A good many grumbled at this duty, and thought it hard—very hard, not to be let sleep all night, after marching all day." The problem persisted throughout, and when Crawford sought to make an example of two sentries who abandoned their posts, his men grumbled. He was reduced to generally rebuking the officers and men and then ordered the officers themselves to make general rounds every thirty minutes when on guard duty and then a circuit of all guards twice a night. In the mornings, an hour before dawn, the officers still had to rouse the men to their sentry posts in anticipation of a dawn attack.[39]

Rose continued, "Order on a march—regularity in point of Duty—and precaution, considering as a body, penetrating into an enemy's country, did seem to be looked upon as matters of mere moonshine."[40] The problem was particularly salient at the army's most vulnerable moments, which increased as the terrain grew rougher and the forest more dense. The trails through Ohio were narrow, originally started as game trails and then occasionally improved by passing Indians, traders, or even small armies. Thickets of nearly impassable thorns and heavy brush crowded around. Crawford's scouts followed a path that led to the burned-out Moravian villages on the Muskingum River, which had become known as Williamson's trail. It played further havoc with Crawford's march order, particularly as the terrain grew worse.[41] The volunteers collapsed into two columns, then one. Creek and ravine crossings became particularly challenging. The banks could be steep, with room for only one man at a time to climb. When everybody rushed pell-mell into the creek bed, the volunteer column would compress and crowd about. Ascending one man at a time, the force would then elongate into single file, further disordering the formation Crawford had attempted to impose. Passing orders from front to rear or information from rear to front became a long, involved task, and the volunteers resembled a caterpillar moving through the woods.[42] Dealing with volunteers, Rose later recorded his frustration. "I found by experience that people who are determined not to see, are the Blindest upon earth."[43] Still, despite the obstacles, the volunteer army kept moving.

Their line of march on May 27 took them across two direct paths to the Moravian towns, their immediate destination, but the army declined to take them, preferring a roundabout direction to avoid detection. Estimating itself to be just eight miles from Gnadenhutten, the middle Moravian town on the eastern branch of the Muskingum, the army bedded down for the night after deciding to dispatch a subordinate detachment of 112 men to the town site in the morning. Since Williamson was to command, this was likely the advance guard and body consisting of companies commanded by Captains John Biggs, Timothy Downie, Ezekiel Rose, Duncan McGihan, and Craig Ritchie.[44]

The next day, Tuesday, some men woke to discover their horses had wandered off. Unable to find them, they set out for home on foot.[45] When it came time to leave the camp for the Gnadenhutten town site, more than two hundred men—nearly half of the volunteer force—decided they should go there, the prior night's plan discarded. There was nothing the officers could do to stop them. By the time they reached the outskirts, about a half mile away, better judgment prevailed, and Crawford halted his command. Williamson, Rose, and the brigade major, Daniel Leet, scouted ahead. Rather than approach the ruin directly, they rode around it, crossing the Muskingum at a ford above town and spotting horse and cow prints scattered about. Finding no people, they returned. Williamson then brought an advance party of about sixty men forward. As if a signal, that small advance sparked the volunteers into a disordered, haphazard rush. The center column sped directly into town while the right and left columns set out for opposite ends. Rose concluded that a desire to loot the destroyed, already-plundered towns drove the men forward: "The pencil of a Hogarth is here wanted to immortalize the ludicrous scene. this undaunted party of Clodhoppers seated on their Meal Baggs and Balancing themselves in rope Stirrups, were kicking into a gallop their miserable nags, sweating under a load of at least 150 Weights provisions besides this huge Rider, who kept pulling the panting animal by a hair halter with but one rein—and steered strait for three half burnt Log houses."[46] Cursing officers could not maintain order as individuals rushed helter-skelter about ruins, even plunging into a pond up to their armpits. Within moments, no one was left to guard the baggage train. Rose concluded that twenty Indians could have brought the entire expedition to collapse by attacking at that moment.

Time and weather had completed the work of destruction that Williamson and his volunteers started in March. Rose noted "the ruins of the lowest house in town were mixed with calcined bones of the burnt bodies of the Indians."[47] James Paul, a volunteer, recorded years later, "At all these Moravian towns silence and desolation reigned; all was desolation . . . there was little, except the extreme lonely aspect of the place."[48] Despite the destruction and looting in March, there were still things to be found. Sundry tools turned up as the volunteers wandered about the ruins. One man found a good garden spade and decided to keep it, proclaiming at least it could be used to bake bread. After exploring the Gnadenhutten site, Crawford's volunteers moved north up the Muskingum and finally made camp at the burned-out ruins of New Schoenbrunn, which some Moravian Indians had abandoned in March just hours ahead of the marauding Americans. Here again, the Americans raiding the area missed some plunder. Rose noted a pond that still contained some of the goods hidden by the Indians before they fled.[49]

That evening, as the volunteers settled in, Major Brenton and Captain Joseph Bean, who commanded a company in Brenton's left wing, decided to reconnoiter the surrounding area. About a quarter mile from the camp, they stumbled upon two Indians, yelled, and shot at both, missing.[50] The shooting and shouting sparked an alarm in the camp. The fact that two officers, and not proper pickets, scouted the area and stumbled on nearby Indians strongly suggests that the poor security practices Rose had complained about since crossing the Ohio River continued. Crawford called an officers council to consider the development and address the problem. Brigadier General Irvine had stressed the importance of speed and surprise in his guidance to the volunteers, their commander, and General Washington. He undoubtedly raised it with Rose as well, as the lieutenant complained mightily about their lack.[51] Now, Crawford and his volunteers knew they had lost both. Indeed, they were more than a week behind their most optimistic schedule, and some men had already been on the move for nearly two weeks since leaving their homes on May 15.

Originally turned into a mounted force for the purposes of moving more quickly, the expedition's horses may have started to become an operational hindrance. Frontier inhabitants generally trained as foot soldiers when called up for militia duty. Crawford's volunteers had little to no experience operating together on horseback, whether as cavalry or mounted infantry.

Neither did Crawford and his officers or, for that matter, Rose. The lieutenant, as impressive as he might be, was an outsider on the frontier, but that did not stop him from raising his concerns about the horses, which he viewed as an encumbrance. In the current state of affairs, each volunteer was left to look after his own mount when in combat. This meant the entire force was momentarily disorganized and incapable of fighting until the horses could be secured properly, each man looking out for himself. Rose proposed a standard military practice for mounted forces: assign some men the responsibility of securing the horses while the others fought. Because surprise was Rose's greatest concern, he urged that the men in the center two columns take on that responsibility for the outer two columns, which would then be free to engage any attackers without first securing their own mounts. The idea proved provocative and "the matter was a good deal altercated," the chief objection coming from those in the center column, who did not want to be reduced to the status of horse holders.[52]

The council rejected what would later become routine practice for cavalry and mounted infantry. But during the Revolution, the United States lacked a well-established cavalry arm or tactical doctrine on which Crawford, much less an ad hoc volunteer force, could rely.[53] Instead, the council ended with a renewed commitment to place pickets around the force for advance warning and have the army stand to arms an hour before dawn. Rose had one other idea, to glean a modest number of men from the expedition and form them into a unit he took to calling the "light horse," as if slouching volunteers on mounts slightly better or less tired than working farm animals could be considered such, and reduce their loads somewhat to turn them into a reconnaissance arm. Because it would spend more time in the saddle and on the move, this scratch unit would be exempt from guard duty. Williamson took up Rose's cause, and the council agreed to it, but "L. and H.," likely Majors Leet and Harrison, who were both personally close to Colonel Crawford, managed to kill it in practice, perhaps contributing to the poor assessment Rose made of them. Still, the expedition proceeded with greater caution.[54]

THE GEOGRAPHY OPENED SOMEWHAT when the expedition renewed its march on May 29, finally allowing it to spread out into
the four columns Crawford had designed. Bogs, creeks, and hills
still broke up the formation occasionally, but the terrain was more
favorable. The expedition made better time, coming across an
occasional sign that Indians had passed by or camped at various
locations on the route. Still, the volunteers alternated paths, preferring to stay off the most-traveled trails between the Sandusky
and the Ohio. While the column moved more rapidly, its winding
route made for slow progress toward the Sandusky. The next day,
the volunteers came across evidence that roughly sixty Indian warriors had moved in the opposite direction, raiding toward the
Ohio just two days prior. Worse, someone, presumably the scouts,
detected tracks for a second party of three Indians keeping pace
just ahead of them since the encampment on the Muskingum.
One had apparently split off and followed the eastbound warriors.
It would be logical to assume the third man would warn them that
the Americans were across the Muskingum in force. Meanwhile,
fires sparked in the woods at different places. Indians were marking the column's general location and direction. This compli-
cated matters considerably. The volunteers now had Indians
ahead of them and a smaller group of Indians behind them, and
both knew roughly where the Americans were. They pressed on,
posting handbills at their campsites declaring they intended to
leave no Indian they found alive.[55]

The next days brought more of the same: woodlands; creeks
that had to be crossed; hills and mires that created defiles where
the army bunched up; bogs that had to be circumnavigated; an
occasional salt lick; thickets that caught on horses, equipment,
and the odd exposed limb; various paths trod by Indians and
traders for years; and several Indian campsites interpreted as way-
points that eastbound Indian war parties had created. Crawford
asked for volunteers to warn the frontier. One man stepped up,
provided that he not go alone. When nobody offered to join him,

the matter was dropped.[56] At the end of the day, the volunteers camped at a spring, where one of their number died and was buried, his initials carved on a tree to mark the spot.[57] Circulating through the camp, Crawford learned that some men were down to five pounds of flour or roughly ten days of rations.

On the morning of Saturday, June 1, the volunteers crossed only the latest in a number of modest rivers and large streams. Rose observed, "Immediately after crossing this midle Fork the road takes Westerly and is very broken, hilly, & full of disagreeable thickets. After passing a small Bottom, we ascended a ridge full of fallen timber several miles long running between N.W. and due North." Five miles on, they encountered another branch of the same river. He complained "you crawl upon an uneven road beset with thickets along the slanting side of a hill," but after plowing through the tangled terrain, the army entered an open river bottom, which "on account of the pleasantness of its situation rather deserved the name of the Elysian fields." The horses, exhausted from their constant trek and making do on limited grass in the forest, could graze a little and drink from the river. So Crawford halted the column and called an officers council.[58]

The Americans, of course, were not the first to take notice of the area's appeal. A major Indian trail ran through it. Crawford sent a reconnaissance party down the road, and it discovered two Indians. The volunteers fired three shots at them but missed. Alarmed, the expedition promptly formed a rectangle, with four companies dividing it into three sections and two of the advance companies posted outside the longer sides. Crawford arranged his men so that everyone faced out, then called another officers council. It was time to make some decisions.

Crawford laid out the situation as he saw it. According to information he had from George Rogers Clark in Kentucky, all of Britain's forces could easily be concentrated within miles of Upper Sandusky in a few days and certainly within the several days that had passed since the volunteers were spotted on May 28. The colonel remained confident they could reach their destination and fight a battle. He was concerned, however, about the lack of

reliable intelligence about their destination. In the event the Indians or British had built blockhouses, the volunteers had no artillery or means of reducing them. A battle would surely result in
wounded, and they had no ready means of transport. Moreover,
securing the route back to the Pennsylvania frontier would also
be challenging. Indians excelled at ambushes and attacking the
fringes of a column. In the event that the volunteers were defeated, both problems would only become worse. That those
questions had not been asked and answered by Irvine and Crawford before the volunteers set out from Mingo Bottom demon-
strates horrendously poor planning beforehand by the local
leaders who agitated for the campaign, particularly Marshel and
Williamson, and by General Irvine, who eventually blessed the
campaign and could not plead ignorance about the need to consider those problems.

Facing these obstacles, Crawford raised the possibility of
changing goals. In his mind, the well-traveled Indian trails
through the bottom suggested villages to their north. By diverting
and attacking those targets, the volunteers could still accomplish
some of their goals while evading the likely enemies gathering at
Sandusky. A scout, Zane, noted that in the past at least one Indian
village had existed to their north. He also indicated they could
follow a less-used trail to reach it.[59] In theory, it was not an entirely
bad idea. To the degree that loot was the goal, finding a closer,
less-well-defended village would not produce as much, but what
plunder was available might be had with considerably lower risk.
Also, simply engaging Native Americans in their own territory
might produce Indian refugees and reduce some of the pressure
on settlers across the Ohio. Finally, such a raid would culminate
farther from the Indian and British forces Crawford argued were
waiting for them at Sandusky and leave the volunteers closer to
home, meaning any wounded would not have to be transported
as far and their existing rations might be sufficient to take them
back across the Ohio. The officers council rejected Crawford's
idea. It was Sandusky or bust. After all, the Wyandot and their
Delaware allies had become implacable American enemies and

were always the intended targets. The council broke up and, no attack having materialized, the men left their defensive positions and resumed the march.

Sunday passed much the same, following winding, muddy trails, dodging bogs, and navigating hills. The army camped on a small stream, a tributary of the Sandusky. It was on the precipice of reaching its goal.[60] On Monday, June 3, the expedition followed the stream to the Sandusky and came across an abandoned Indian village, the first reminder that Indian towns were not permanent locations on a map. The woodlands of eastern and central Ohio also began to thin before everything fell away into one great grassland. Aesthetically, Rose was pleased with what he saw: "the aspect of these plains is exceedingly pleasant, interspersed with groups of trees forming Islands. The different kinds of grass indicate the different qualities of the ground underneath. Its height is 3 1/2 feet." He took the opportunity to resurrect the idea of a body of light horse, which Williamson again pressed on his behalf. This time Crawford agreed. Dr. Knight also liked what he saw, particularly as it related to their mounted force: "there are a great many extensive plains in that country: The woods in general grow very thin, and free from brush and underwood; so that light horsemen may advance a considerable distance before an army without being much exposed to the enemy."[61]

Looks can be deceiving, however. Rose and Knight were being exposed to the plain for the first time. Missionary David Zeisberger, who with his congregation on the Muskingum had been forcibly removed to a reservation on the Sandusky by the Wyandot and western Delaware the previous fall, saw bleaker terrain: "We went through a perfect plain, where there is nothing but grass, which is so high and long that on horseback a man can hardly see over it, only here and there a little clump of bushes. No hill, much less a mountain, in sight, but all the land is flat, consequently it is a moist soil, since the rain-water can not run off."[62] Zeisberger and his congregation went on to discover that the grass was nutrient poor and made for poor grazing; their cattle herds died off almost entirely in the months that followed. It meant the same for Crawford's exhausted horses, which would not fully replenish themselves as they approached the Sandusky River.

The grassland made it possible to see from horizon to horizon, save for an occasional copse of trees, but the tall grass also hid the little rivulets and minor folds in the ground that created bogs of a sort. Worse, the grass was tall enough to hide modest-sized bodies of warriors. Horses might be able to move swiftly, but they could also be seen more easily than someone crouching. (How quickly the depleted mounts in Crawford's expedition could move was a separate matter.) Moreover, by staying in the grass and following slight depressions in the ground, men afoot could move relatively unseen. Thus, it would be just as easy for Indians to surprise the Americans by relying on concealment as for the Americans to surprise the Indians by relying on allegedly superior speed.

Showers passed through in the afternoon as the men rode north through the grasslands. A little over nine miles after breaking from the woods to the plain, they crossed a large Indian trail. Rose concluded it was a warriors path, hinting at fresh tracks that made it possible to distinguish the route from a cattle path. Just beyond that, Crawford and his men settled in around a spring about six in the evening. After dark, Crawford called another officers council. He wanted to consider options for attacking the Wyandot village of Upper Sandusky, which was within a day's march, or so he thought. First, they could march through the night and assault the town directly in the morning. This was closest to General Irvine's recommendation, although the Americans were nearer to their target than Irvine wanted. The second option was to remain in place overnight and continue the march as normal—scouting ahead, security on the flanks, and prepared for battle—on Tuesday, June 4. Crawford was unfamiliar with the region and believed they would need daylight to conduct a proper reconnaissance before attacking. (Rose believed Crawford favored the latter approach). Most of his officers agreed, arguing that they might end up shooting one another in the dark should

they stumble across the town before dawn and that any white prisoners with the Indians would be killed in the dark.[63] How the second option addressed their concern about prisoners went
unaddressed, but in the end, the council decided to march out
on June 4, still headed cautiously for Upper Sandusky.

In the early hours of June 4, the camped Americans heard the
distant discharge of cannon. Michael Walters, a volunteer serving
in Captain John Beason's company, counted six shots. But, the
night was damp from the prior day's showers, and fog rolled
across the ground, so the distance and number were difficult to
judge. The cannon fire impressed at least a few Americans as a
summons to rally.[64] It should have dispelled any remaining hope
among the Americans that they might surprise the Indians along
the Sandusky.

BRIG. GEN. WILLIAM IRVINE.

Wm Irvine

Figure 1. Continental Brigadier General William Irvine. Irvine was captured during the invasion of Canada and exchanged in 1778. By 1782, he was serving as Commander of the Western Department. He used his influence to help swing command of the Sandusky campaign to Colonel William Crawford. (*New York Public Library*)

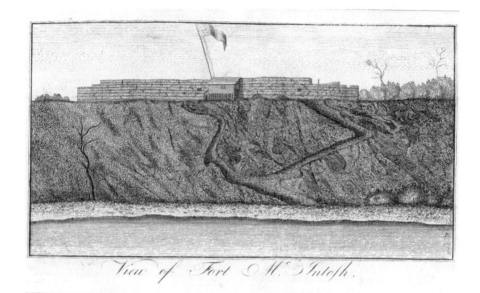

Figure 2. View of Fort McIntosh. Scottish born Brigadier General Lachlan
McIntosh served as Commander of the Western Department from 1778–1779.
He planned to attack Detroit and built Fort McIntosh on the Beaver River and
then Fort Laurens on the Muskingum River as supply depots in late 1778.
Simon Girty helped coordinate a siege of Fort Laurens in the winter and it
was abandoned in 1779. After Dr. Knight's escape from his Indian captor and
three weeks on the run, American hunters found the famished, dehydrated,
and suffering doctor and brought him into Fort McIntosh on July 4. (*New York
Public Library*)

Figure 3. Battle of Sandusky by Frank Halbedel. Unlike the larger battles on the seaboard, Revolutionary War battles west of the Appalachians drew little attention from artists. Images created in the nineteenth century reflected the artistic styles of their time, often creating overly dramatic and inaccurate portrayals. Battle Island was a modest hill notable primarily for its trees, while men fought primarily on foot. (*Wyandot County Historical Society*)

Figure 4. Burning of Col. Crawford by Frank Halbedel. Dr. John Knight's description of Colonel Crawford's execution made it possible to illustrate the scene in vivid, lurid, and accurate detail. Halbedel's painting corresponds with other descriptions of prisoner burnings after the battle. (*Wyandot County Historical Society*)

CRAWFORD'S BATTLE-FIELD.

Figure 5. Crawford's Battle-Field, colored etching, from *The Great West: Containing Narratives of the Most Important and Interesting Events in Western History* by Henry Howe (New York: Geo. F. Tuttle, 1857). The original caption reads, "The large tree on the right of the engraving, and others in the vicinity, even to the present day, show marks of the bullets." In the early nineteenth century, missionaries and white farmers moved into the Sandusky River basin. They had the opportunity to speak with elderly Native Americans who might have participated in the battle and knew approximately where events took place. Familiarity with the ground worked against misrepresentations of Battle Island. (*New York Public Library*)

Figure 6, left. Crawford monument. Much of the area associated with the Battle of Upper Sandusky is privately owned and actively farmed. It has been so for centuries, but residents in the area have worked to commemorate Revolutionary War events in northwest Ohio by building monuments in publicly accessible areas as near to events as possible. The site of Colonel Crawford's execution is noted in a nearby cemetery outside Crawford, Ohio. (*Author*)

Figure 7, right. Olentangy Battle monument. The skirmish at Olentangy near the edge of the plains, which was ended by a sudden rainstorm, is marked on a public right-of-way north of the Olentangy River and southeast of Bucyrus, Ohio. Lieutenant Colonel Williamson and his men stopped to water their horses when they were attacked by pursuing Native Americans and some of Butler's Rangers. (*Author*)

Figure 8. The battlefield today. Battle Island was marked primarily by a grove of trees that covered its slopes and contrasted with the surrounding plains. The slope is quite gentle. Grasslands have been replaced with cultivated fields, eliminating the tall grass that combatants from both sides used for concealment while tree lines used as wind-breaks and border markers have replaced groves. (*Author*)

Figure 9. The battlefield today. From a distance, the gentle slopes of Battle Island are more visible. The copse of trees that crowned Battle Island distinguished it as a memorable place for Lieutenant Rose and his men to offload
their equipment so they could move more quickly north toward Dunquat's village. (*Author*)

THREE

Battle Island

SOME THIRTY MILES NORTH OF UPPER SANDUSKY, an American trader named Johnathan Leith who was working for British business interests breakfasted with a passing Frenchman, saddled his horse, and loaded his packhorses with goods from British traders at Detroit when he heard cannon fire in the distance. The Frenchman, most likely a Detroit-based interpreter for the British named Francois LeVilliers, "clapped his hand to his breast and said 'I shall be there before the battle is begun.'"[1] Then he rushed south.

Leith was an American, seized by the Delaware in central Ohio in 1774 while representing the interests of a Pittsburgh-based fur trader. Released under the terms of the treaty ending Dunmore's War the same year, he resumed the business of hunting and trading furs. Then the Shawnee kidnapped him in 1776. They sold him to the Wyandot, who set him free as an adopted member of the Delaware nation. Once again, Leith resumed hunting and trading before making his way to Detroit in 1777. Lieutenant Governor Henry Hamilton tried to enlist him as an interpreter in British service, but Leith simply wanted to resume trading and sought a pass to do so. Hamilton denied it, but Leith's relations with the Ohio tribes led them to use him for their own purposes. Hamilton eventually relented, and Leith began trading on the Lower Sandusky River before returning to the Delaware nation, this time on the Muskingum River. There he married a white woman kidnapped as a child by an Ohio tribe and then moved in with the Moravian communities. He was with them when the Wyandot forcibly relocated the Moravians to the Sandusky in fall 1781. Leith was unable to continue trading on his own but secured a position as an agent for British merchants in Detroit. This is how he found himself among the Wyandot at Upper Sandusky in 1782 when the Americans came calling.[2]

The Ohio Indians, of course, had tracked the Sandusky expedition since before it crossed the Ohio River on May 24. The local Wyandot and Delaware kept a close eye on Leith as the Americans advanced. He was no spy but still learned from the Indians "every evening where the army was encamped."[3] On June 2, he was informed that the Americans were about fifteen miles away and immediately began packing to move his cattle and goods downriver. He and his hands set out at first light the next morning. Just three miles outside of town, he encountered British Captain Matthew Elliott, whom DePeyster had sent to "command" the Indians, making his way to Upper Sandusky. Twelve miles and several hours later, he crossed paths with Captain Caldwell and his detachment of Butler's Rangers also moving south. They promptly relieved him of his cattle. By evening, Leith was just fourteen miles south of Lower Sandusky when he made his camp. As he prepared his supper, the Frenchman rode up and announced his plans to share the camp overnight, ostensibly to protect Leith, his men, and his wares from Indians.[4]

WHILE LEITH'S FRENCHMAN made his way south on Tuesday, June 4, Crawford and his men roused themselves amid a thick fog. Because it had rained the afternoon before, they discharged their weapons by company to burn off any damp powder. After loading horses, the volunteers set out from their campsite. In northwestern Ohio, the Sandusky River makes long zig-zags from east to west before turning north toward Sandusky Bay and Lake Erie. There are significant disagreements about Crawford's exact route, but the volunteers generally stayed south of the east-west portion and crossed several large tributaries. The scouts disagreed whether they flowed into the Sandusky River or the Scioto, highlighting American uncertainty about the region and its terrain.[5] Seven miles into their march, the volunteers discovered the remains of a village, which the ever-present Lieutenant Rose concluded was one hurriedly built by the Moravian Indians the previous autumn but subsequently abandoned and burned. For all he knew, the former inhabitants might have been the victims of some of the very volunteers marching around him. Just beyond that, they came across still more empty cabins, likely belonging to the Wyandot. Farther on, they climbed a hill, where a path to the Shawnee towns joined the road to Upper Sandusky before continuing north parallel to, and on the west side of, the river as it bent toward Lake Erie.[6] Just beyond the hill they arrived at another town site, their intended target. The Wyandot had already abandoned it. Rose recorded, "Here some murmur arose among the men & near 100 combined not to proceed any farther, as they thought the Indians were moved to Lower Sandusky, because no signs of anything living was discernible about this place."[7] After the scouts announced that rumors indicated the town had moved two miles farther down the river, the men agreed to go that far.

Williamson requested to lead fifty men two miles farther and burn the town he believed was just downriver. Clearly, in Williamson's mind the Indians had fled. Otherwise he would have requested a sufficient number of men to engage in battle. It was a reasonable conclusion, but Crawford was unwilling to divide his command. A quick officers' call decided to press on a bit. Five more miles passed with no sign of Indians before Crawford called a break, giving the men and horses a chance to eat and rest while he took the measure of his troops and their inclinations.[8] Lieutenant Rose posted his light horse, now constituting forty men in two companies, around the perimeter and explored some nearby woods, essentially tackling the weak security he had complained about since the campaign's beginning.

The surliness of earlier in the morning had grown, and a majority of the expedition was ready to turn back. With no sign of Indians, towns, or cattle, there was little chance of engaging in battle or seizing plunder for the return home. Worse, some men complained that their supplies were growing short.[9] After circulating among the volunteers, Crawford called a council. Before it could fully assemble, he ordered Rose to take some of his men farther down the Sandusky to see what he could. Simply, it would not do if they turned around now and the enemy was over the next hill or around the next river bend. Williamson, showing every sign of wanting to continue, took Rose aside and told him he had been assured the Wyandot village was just a few more miles off.[10] While Rose and one of his volunteer light horse companies rode forward, the council commenced. Officers were of different minds. Some, like Williamson, wanted to continue. Others had concluded from their fruitless morning marches that the Indians they hoped to find had moved farther down the Sandusky, perhaps all the way to Lower Sandusky, which was an additional forty miles.[11] For them, it was time to go home. And so the debate continued.

While the officers talked and the volunteers milled about, Lieutenant Rose led twenty-four men north. They moved slowly at first. After about a mile and a half, he stopped in a copse of woods on a modest hill for his men to deposit their baggage and supplies. He wanted to travel light and move quickly. Some three miles into his scout and approaching the edge of some woods, Rose's leading men, perhaps one or more of the scouts, spotted three cabin roofs in the distance. Then several things happened at once.

From a depression or ravine hidden by the tall grass, a group of Indians rose from ambush and fired a volley into Rose's men.[12] Rose also caught sight of a "party of Indians upon my right along the edge of a wood, and a large Body trying with the utmost velocity to gain my rear."[13] Captain Caldwell, his rangers, and just over forty of the Lake Indians from Detroit were among the two hundred ambushers.[14] It was about two o'clock.[15]

Rose immediately retreated with three aims in mind. First, he wanted to alert Crawford and the main body that they had discovered the Indian town and encountered resistance. Doing so would focus minds quickly in the council, which he knew to be divided and confused, and prevent the expedition from being surprised. Ideally, Crawford and his officers would be able to shake out the men in some sort of battle formation given enough time. Second, he needed to ensure that his own small force was not cut off from Crawford, which he did not think likely given the numbers he had seen and the openness of the country. Still, Rose could not be sure how many more Indians were out there, as yet unseen. Third, he hoped to recover the baggage and supplies his party had deposited on the wooded hill to his rear.[16]

Rose's withdrawal was orderly. He dispatched two riders, including William Midkirk, to Crawford on the fastest mounts to raise the alarm and report what little he knew.[17] Then he ordered a second group of men to return to the wooded hill where they had deposited their supplies and wait for him. Finally, he dispersed the remainder of his men across the plain, where they fired an occasional shot at the Indians and backpedaled more slowly toward the hill themselves. The lieutenant hoped that by slowing the Indian movements, he could buy time, so he continually moved his men about in the fields as they pulled back. "[B]y dispersing my men [I] suspended the ennemy's attention" while the messengers rode to Crawford. As the minutes passed, "I continued forming my men upon eminences and then again dispersing them over the plains, [so] that I gained a good Deal of time."[18]

It was as close as the lieutenant could come to a fighting withdrawal with the modest number of men at hand. It worked, and Captain Caldwell of Butler's Rangers was struck early in the fight by an American bullet, which passed through one leg and lodged in the other.[19] Command of the rangers passed to Lieutenant John Turney as Caldwell retired from the field.

By the time Rose reached the wooded hill where he had stopped just a few hours earlier and reunited with some of his men, he could see fifty "naked & painted" Indians on the plain before him. (They undoubtedly continued to wear breechcloths and leggings.) He engaged them from the hill. Farther back, however, in Crawford's direction, Rose could see a larger body of Indians still maneuvering around him and into some woods to his rear, threatening to cut off his small party.[20] During the retreat, Rose noted a morass to his left, which made the woods to his rear the only route of withdrawal. It was a perilous moment.

Back at the main body, Rose's messengers galloped in just as the officers council was breaking up.[21] Participants in the council left no written record of its decision, but the speed with which the expedition mounted and headed for Rose and the Wyandot village indicates that it had decided to continue advancing. Two factors likely contributed to that course of action. Williamson had consistently pressed for it, and Crawford did not want to return as a failed commander. As the expedition moved forward, it crossed more grasslands and heard the distant gunfire of Rose's men exchanging shots with the Indians. Eventually, the volunteers came within sight of the woods between them and the hill where Rose was making his stand. Native American warriors were already moving about among those trees.

On the hill, Rose recorded observing Crawford's men advance into the woods behind him, which would mean he had waited on the hill, despite not knowing what the main body was doing behind him. Lieutenant Turney of Butler's Rangers similarly reported to Major DePeyster at Detroit that the Americans made a stand on the wooded hill, which "had every advantage of us as to situation of ground as people could possibly wish for." Dr. Knight with the main body reported "the rest of the light horse," pre-sumably the men Rose had left behind as vedettes when he set out on his scout, joined it before it advanced into the woods.[22]

Whereas the main battle had been between Rose's few men and roughly two hundred Indians and some eighty rangers across the plains north of Rose's hill in the early afternoon, the arrival of the remaining Americans shifted the focus to the woods on the eastern edge of the hill and south of it, which Crawford's men were approaching. The volunteers came on at more than a walk but less than a gallop and quickly dismounted after they were fired on.[23] Angus McCoy, under Captain Charles Bilderback in McLelland's right wing, wrote, "giving us the signal, we each Mounted and went to Meet them as fast as we could, thier was one Indean who did out run His comrades to Meet us. Be he was the first Killed. we dismounted and endeavoured to screen our selves behind the few remaining trees and let them advance on us. The play of humane destruction began."[24] With Crawford's ar-rival, the two groups were reunited, and fighting became general and "hot" by four o'clock.[25] Rose's wooded copse, which rose like an island from a surrounding sea of grass, forever after became known as Battle Island. It was the central American defensive po-sition. Fighting took place in the woods and fields around it.

The exact positions of volunteers and Native Americans are uncertain. Assuming the volunteers engaged the Indians in march order, which they had used to form defensive positions on June 1, Williamson's advance body of five companies with Captain Biggs's company in the lead would have made first contact, mov-ing on the Indians Rose had watched trying to cut him off in the woods to his south. Major Brenton commanded four companies on the left, Major McLelland led four of the larger companies on the right, and Colonel Gattis brought up the rear with five more companies.[26] The expedition fought its way onto the slopes of Bat-tle Island, pushing aside the Indians between them and Rose.

THE LOCAL INDIANS knew Crawford's main body was coming and reacted, but historians disagree over who authored the warrior response. British Captain Matthew Elliott's role is murky. He was sent south with instructions to command or direct Indian movements. But that raises the question of his ability to do so. British and Loyalist material places him in command, which some modern historians have followed.[27] But it was in the self-interest of British authorities to think of themselves, and represent themselves, as commanding Indian actions. In truth, throughout the war, British abilities to "direct" Indian actions were decidedly limited, a fact not always grasped on the other side of the Appalachians, much less London. Simply, getting the Native Americans involved in the war was a matter of supporting Indian self-interest, incentivizing behavior with rewards, enabling behavior with supplies, suppressing tribal conflicts, and cajoling various tribes to act. Because each Indian nation had its own strengths, weaknesses, and concept of self-interest, authorities at Detroit, and British officers in the field, whether from the Indian Department or the army, were often reduced to manipulating Indian leaders. It was a two-way street. Indian leaders had proven themselves quite adept at manipulating British authorities. The irony was that everyone knew it but downplayed the fact in order to move in a common direction. Indian-British relations were, in effect, a constantly evolving series of spoken and unspoken negotiations.

Elliott was no exception to this fundamental reality in British-Indian relations. Indeed, when he arrived at the Moravian villages in summer 1781, Elliott pitched a tent and began trading, his prewar occupation. (He essentially bought Moravian goods, animals, and foodstuffs at fire-sale prices, as the alternatives were looting by Dunquat's Wyandot and his allies or abandonment when the Moravians were forced to depart.) It was clear to the missionaries that Dunquat, and not Captain Elliott, was in charge of events on the Muskingum and the Sandusky that fall and winter. Elliott specifically denied any decision-making authority in the process of removing the Moravian Indians from the Muskingum.[28] So in no real way could he command or direct Indian movements on the Sandusky. At best, he could attempt to coordinate among multiple tribes: the two most important in the region, the Delaware and Wyandot, plus a smattering of Lake Indians who had come with him from Detroit. But Dunquat, Hopocan, and his war leader, Wingenund, were making the combat decisions on June 4. When they opened the battle, they had just two hundred Wyandot, Delaware, and Mingo warriors in the immediate vicinity, plus the seventy or so British rangers under Captain Caldwell and a smattering of forty to fifty Chippewa, Ottawa, Potawatomi, and Mingo who had come down with Caldwell and Elliott from the areas around Detroit.[29] Unfortunately, Indian leaders did not keep a copious correspondence with their British counterparts, so their decisions have to be teased out from their actions.

Indian scouts had tracked Crawford's men all the way from the Ohio River. As Leith indicated, they knew where the volunteer expedition was at the end of every day. That meant Dunquat and Hopocan had time to plan their reception. Although they could not predict Crawford's reaction to the abandoned towns he initially found on the Sandusky, the Indians knew from placards left behind by the volunteers that they intended to kill every man, woman, and child they encountered. Gnadenhutten provided ample reason to take the Americans at their word. Dunquat, Hopocan, and other Indian leaders could not know that General Irvine had engineered Crawford's election to command in the hope of restraining the volunteers and avoiding a repeat of that massacre.

So when Rose began scouting ahead, the Indians likely interpreted his advance as the opening move of a do-or-die battle and were well prepared for him. Hopocan, Wingenund, and the Delaware, accompanied by the British Indian agent Simon Girty, were in front. They likely sprang the trap on Rose early in the battle. Then they took the lead in surrounding him. Crawford's men thus crashed into them as the expedition moved forward to Rose's relief.

It would have been obvious quickly that Rose's small party was not the main body of American volunteers. Whereas the Americans and British both mentioned actions by the Delaware and Lake Indians, references to the Wyandot are curiously sparse. Yet they constituted the bulk of Indians living on the Sandusky and should have numerically outnumbered the Delaware and Lake Indians combined. As a result, we are forced to surmise Wyandot actions by filling in the blanks and acknowledging the dominance Dunquat had demonstrated in leading a multitribal group of Indians on the Muskingum during summer 1781.[30]

In the battle's opening minutes, Dunquat apparently held his Wyandot back, waiting to see how things developed and making it easier to keep his warriors between the Americans, the new Wyandot town, and its surrounding fields and stores, not to mention the women and children who had evacuated. At a meeting with Elliott early in the battle, he reportedly told the British Indian agent, dressed in the full regalia of an army captain, that he intended to take control of Battle Island before the Americans did. Elliott cautioned against splitting the Indian force but eventually gave in to the Wyandot leader.[31] As a result, while the Delaware moved through scattered trees and high grass around Rose's flanks, Dunquat's warriors advanced head-on and were likely the "naked & painted" men Rose drew into the plains before him. It was a classic encirclement and might well have worked had Crawford not responded to the messengers from Rose so quickly.

BATTLE ISLAND WAS NOT ROUND or symmetrical. Wooded spurs along the hillsides stretched away in the front and rear. Another thin stretch of scattered trees on the eastern end connected to a larger wood across open grassland. Combat did not take place in traditional European fashion, with disciplined, well-ordered lines of infantrymen fighting as units, advancing across open ground in several ranks, trading volley fire, and charging with bayonets.

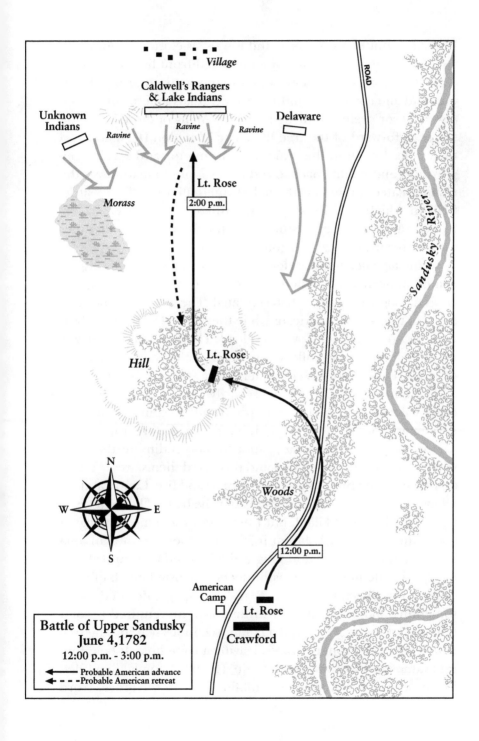

Village

Caldwell's Rangers
& Lake Indians

Unknown
Indians

Delaware

Ravine   *Ravine*   *Ravine*

ROAD

Morass

Lt. Rose

2:00 p.m.

Sandusky River

Hill   Lt. Rose

N

W   E

Woods

S

12:00 p.m.

American
Camp
☐   Lt. Rose

**Battle of Upper Sandusky
June 4, 1782**
12:00 p.m. - 3:00 p.m.

Crawford

⟵——— Probable American advance
⟵- - - Probable American retreat

Instead, volunteers dispersed and fought as clusters or individuals. There was a semblance of an ordered front line, largely because Crawford's men arrived as a semiorganized group, but it was fluid and constantly shifting as individuals sought cover, concealment, or preferred firing locations. Many of those lay in the tall grass forward of the tree line. The Wyandot, Delaware, and their allies fought in the same way, moving forward seeking opportunity and pulling back to rest or resupply. In many ways, the result created a number of ruleless duels all around the battlefield in which individuals crept, rushed, fired, retreated, reloaded, and fired again until they hit their man, sometimes without regard to what was going on elsewhere.

In the advance body under Williamson, Captain John Biggs's company, normally assigned to lead, faced Indians in the grasslands through which Rose had retreated. The tall grass concealed many of the Native Americans while they moved forward, only to pop up, fire, and duck down to reload. The grass, of course, was no protection against bullets. Americans at the edge of the wood were more visible but had greater cover available behind trees and could thus reload in some security. Daniel Canon and two other volunteers looked for an opportunity to combine the two, cover and concealment, by climbing into the treetops, from where they could more easily spot Indians hiding in the grass while being somewhat hidden and protected themselves.[32] When an Indian raised himself up to see targets and fire, Canon and his fellows would shoot. He remarked after the battle, "I do not know how many Indians I killed, but I never saw the same head again above the grass after I shot at it."[33] Below them, John Gunsaula had fouled his weapon and sang while he tried to clear it.[34] The day grew quite hot, and the volunteers exhausted much of their water. John Sherrard, also in Biggs's company, decided to do something about it. Setting his rifle down, he ventured beyond the edge of the grove toward a fallen tree in his search. The tree had keeled over from the roots, leaving a large hole. It held foul rainwater, but that would have to do. He drank some, then filled his canteen and hat before scrambling back to the grove. Word spread and he made several trips to the fallen tree to refill multiple canteens, under fire much of the time once his actions were detected.[35]

Captain Craig Ritchie's company was normally assigned to the left flank of Williamson's advance body. His company lieutenant was Francis Dunlavy.[36] During the day, Dunlavy engaged in one of those duels veterans remembered. He focused his attention and fired on a very large Indian, whom he later concluded was "Big Captain Johnny." The man was tall enough to convince some whites he stood a full seven feet. The two men squared off on opposite sides of a newly fallen tree with enough leaves on it to conceal what lay behind. Despite his size, Captain Johnny crept close enough to leap from cover and throw his tomahawk at the volunteer. Fortunately for Dunlavy, he missed.[37]

Captain Johnny was likely a Mekoche Shawnee leader named Kekewepelethy, a hardline opponent of accommodating American expansion north and west of the Ohio River. The Shawnee rose to prominence as an early promoter of a pan-Indian movement to resist American settlement north of the Ohio River.[38] After the Revolution, he was a constant presence at treaty negotiations with the Americans and then a staunch ally of the Shawnee leader Blue Jacket during the wars of the Northwest Territory, when just such a coalition came together.[39] The bulk of Shawnee warriors had not arrived on the battlefield just yet, but Kekewepelethy's presence is an excellent reminder that Wyandot and Delaware were not the only Native American nations facing the American volunteers on June 4.[40]

Dunlavy too led an interesting life after the war, pursing an education in Virginia, teaching school, founding a Latin school near Cincinnati, serving in the legislature of the Northwestern Territory and then in the body that wrote Ohio's constitution, practicing law, and eventually becoming justice of the Court of Common Pleas for the First Circuit in Ohio. He died in 1839.[41]

Fighting elsewhere was equally tense. Captain Ezekiel Rose, who was normally posted on Williamson's right, took a bullet in the chest. Farther down the line, the men under Major McLelland, commanding the right wing of the main body, also faced an aggressive adversary, as more of the Native Americans arriving on the battlefield filtered around Crawford's force to that side of Battle Island.[42] Captain James Munn was wounded and lay in the tall grass beyond Battle Island's tree line. His leg was broken and his face lacerated, apparently by a knife or a tomahawk. The volunteers watched as Indians crept toward him to finish the job. Finally, William Brady from Munn's company mounted his horse and rushed out, hoisted the captain aboard, and made it back to the American lines. The surgeon set Munn's leg and bandaged his face.[43]

Most of those who moved past the tree line in McLelland's command fought as the Indians did, staying low through the grass only to rise up, shoot, and duck back into concealment to reload. But Angus McCoy, in Captain Bilderback's company, opted to remain upright in plain sight, firing, reloading, and firing again. Naturally, he drew attention, but he survived the day with his clothes shot full of holes. McCoy later recalled, "A merciful Providence preserved my flesh."[44]

On the left, Major Brenton pushed too far forward, stretching and thinning his line. Captain Joseph Bean, who commanded one of his companies, was quickly wounded.[45] Pressure from the Native Americans on that flank forced Brenton to pull back to the relative safety of the slopes and contract the line.[46]

In the rear, Colonel Gattis and his volunteers had a rough time too as the Indians worked to complete their encirclement, perhaps moving past McLelland's flank.[47] Maneuvering there was easier than in the west in part due to the marshy ground Rose had noticed earlier during his rearguard action across the grassland before Battle Island. Captain John Hoagland was killed outright. In his company, Mike Myers took cover behind a tree. Bark exploded in his face, leading him to peer around to see who had taken the shot. He spotted an adversary some twenty feet away crouched behind a white walnut tree. About three feet from the ground, the tree forked. When the Indian rose into position in order to shoot again, Myers fired first and killed him. He later

noticed "a large number of squaws" moving behind a line of warriors, stripping the American dead of their clothing and retrieving any wounded Indians.[48]

Historian C. W. Butterfield related a tale of Philip Smith, who
claimed that bark flew several times from the tree he was hiding
behind. Rather than move, Smith kept peeking around looking
for his assailant. Finally spotting him, Smith killed the Indian
after seven attempts. Waiting a bit, he then crawled into the grass
looking for the body. It had already been dragged off, but he discovered a blood trail leading away from the battlefield. Smith was
later wounded in the elbow.[49]

The Indians facing Gattis were most likely Delaware and perhaps a smattering of the warriors from Lake nations who arrived
with Captains Elliott and Caldwell. They had been on the move
the longest and were best positioned to reach the rear of the
American force. It would have been natural for Dunquat to reinforce them as his Wyandot moved forward and extended their
circle, freeing up warriors posted on the sides of the hill to move
toward the rear. They were surely tiring, but the Indians pressed
the fight, getting close enough to scalp at least one man. Michael
Walters, in Captain Beason's company, recorded "they could not
Break our lines tho they often attempted to Do it."[50] Gattis and his
men held their ground, protecting the route over which the Americans had advanced and their main line of retreat. Of particular
concern was a skirt of woods connecting Battle Island with a main
Indian battle position in a more distant wood. It was important to
clear those woods and secure the rear, but Gattis's volunteers were
reluctant to push into the trees and force the issue. Rose joined
Gattis there in the evening, writing that the colonel had moved at
least some of his forces to the right, likely to connect with McLelland. In his absence, someone, probably Major Harrison, who had
stymied attempts to maintain a mounted force of light horse before, ordered the remainder of Rose's troops to dismount.[51] Finally, as the sun fell, the colonel managed to get his men moving,
and they eventually cleared the skirt of woods, forcing them to retreat "Across a big Glade."[52] Angus McCoy wrote of one quick

charge in his pension application. Chronologically in his application, it occurred on June 4, but as we will see later, it may have happened on June 5. In this case, we will follow his pension application, which lines up reasonably well with Gattis's efforts to clear the southern skirt of woods at the end of June 4:

> Finding that the Indeans were concealed in the long grass, Daniel Leet Mounted his Horse and as he passed me Looked me in the face said follow me. I imeadieately gave the same invitation to those around me who were on foot. I took after Leet who rode between us on a Canter and a Gallop and I suppose between fifteen and twenty after me. We routed them in Groups out of the grass. In this dareing Manuver in their Consternation not a gun was fired at us Until Leet wheeled to the left, at which time two Indeans discharged at Leet. I saw his Horse bounce as if Mortally wounded (but neither injured). Our pass was so quick we had no time to fire on them, and a Kind of Providence prevented them. We supposed that we passed at least one half of the Indian line.[53]

Once they were across the clearing, the Indians turned and the lines stabilized on opposite sides of the open ground. One of McCoy's friends was wounded and lent the volunteer his rifle and shot at that point. McCoy noted the growing problem of shortages and confessed, "I felt my self stouter being prepared with my additional stock of Ammunition." The shooting finally died off with that final action.

THROUGHOUT THE FIGHTING, Crawford was constantly on the move, exposing himself to danger and maintaining his composure, as if to lead his men by example in the demonstration of personal courage. He was on the front lines enough for a bullet to shatter his powder horn.[54] In Crawford's frenetic activity, however, Lieutenant Rose detected micromanagement, with the resulting poor performance of the volunteer expedition as a

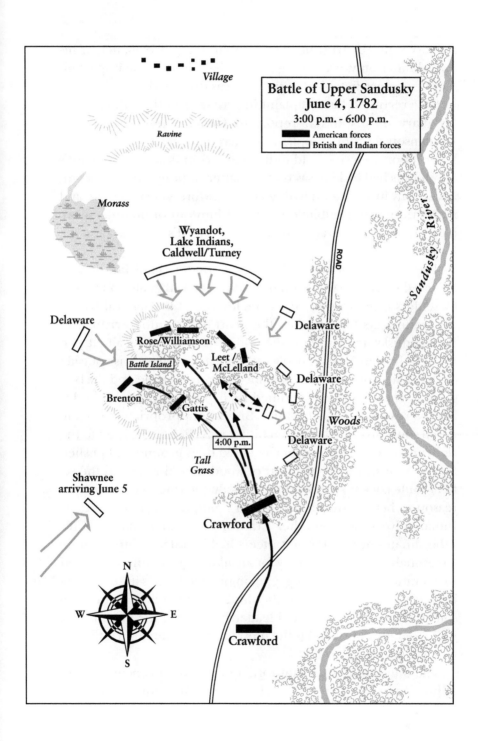

Village

Ravine

**Battle of Upper Sandusky
June 4, 1782**
3:00 p.m. - 6:00 p.m.

■ American forces
□ British and Indian forces

Morass

Wyandot,
Lake Indians,
Caldwell/Turney

ROAD

Sandusky River

Delaware

Delaware

Rose/Williamson

Battle Island

Leet /
McLelland

Delaware

Brenton

Gattis

Woods

4:00 p.m.

Delaware

Tall
Grass

Shawnee
arriving June 5

Crawford

N
W   E
S

Crawford

military unit: "by trusting everything to the performance of his own abilities only, everything was but half done." The impact on morale was predictable: "Everybody was disgusted."[55]

Rose recorded his complaint in private after the battle, not in his diary or his initial report to General Irvine. Similarly, Williamson did not complain of micromanagement in his brief letter report to Irvine, and individual accounts and recollections of veterans had little to say on the matter, although they were not necessarily in a position to detect it. Crawford's eventual fate and martyrization put public criticism of him out of bounds, so we have only Rose's characterization of Crawford's command on the fourth to hand.

The colonel's actions might speak louder. Thus far, he had achieved several of the operational and tactical goals set for him by settlers clamoring for the expedition and by General Irvine. The volunteers had reached the heart of Wyandot territory on the Sandusky and brought the Ohio tribes to battle, albeit perhaps inadvertently. They had weathered a tactical surprise outside of Dunquat's town, responded quickly, seized and cleared the best ground available, then solidified their position on it. When his left overextended itself, Major Brenton appropriately surrendered some ground to shorten his lines. As fighting shifted to the right and rear, the volunteers had held their ground and pushed Native Americans out of a skirt of woods that threatened the retreat route back up the Sandusky. Finally, the volunteers had every reason to believe they had inflicted multiple casualties on their Indian adversaries. Whether Crawford had micromanaged his subordinates or not, the volunteers had handled affairs on June 4 reasonably well, particularly for an ad hoc group unaccustomed to operating as a unit or engaging in pitched battles in such numbers. It is unlikely that all these things happened randomly; despite Crawford's half-hearted leadership during the march west, his battlefield command is the most logical explanation. Still, victory was far from certain.

The question before Crawford and his volunteers at the end of June 4 was how to proceed. He had several factors to consider.

Whereas the general and his hand-picked colonel understood the need for surprise to maximize the odds of a victory, that was lost on May 28, if not before. To the degree that some of the volunteers anticipated a simple, unopposed raid on the Sandusky Indians to destroy crops, burn houses, and plunder towns, they were surely to be disappointed. It was obvious at the end of June 4 that the Indians had ample time to remove anything of value. If any volunteers hoped to repeat the Gnadenhutten massacre, their dreams were dashed. Thus, at least one reason for the campaign and one anticipated advantage over any Indian defenders had evaporated. Moreover, the men and horses were tired, having been on the move since setting out for Mingo Bottom in early to mid-May. Surliness among the volunteers that very morning almost unraveled the entire campaign. Food, water, and ammunition were growing scarce. Empty knapsacks and stale water from dirty puddles at the foot of overturned trees would not sustain the volunteers much longer. Worse, the men had fired off much of their powder and shot. Poor fire discipline was a problem the entire march. There was no supply train from which to replenish the dwindling amount each man brought with him. Finally, the Americans had no prospects for reinforcement, while the Sandusky tribes had every reason to expect more Native American warriors to arrive from all points of the compass.

Oddly, there is no evidence that Crawford or his officers decided on a future course of action in the night. Instead, they settled for the status quo. The men slept on their arms and lit fires at the outer edges of their lines to illuminate the approaches and prevent surprise. There is some indication that Crawford may have adjusted his forces to straighten and rebalance his perimeter, but a quarter-mile gap remained on the right where the Indians had pressed McLelland all afternoon.[56] Losses for the day included two men killed outright and three who died of their wounds overnight. Nineteen wounded survived the night, but three of them had mortal wounds.[57]

As the firing died off into an occasional desultory shot and the sun faded out of sight, the Indians withdrew some distance but maintained pickets around Battle Island. They too lit fires around the perimeter, then offered up occasional war whoops and shots. Neither side would be able to use the darkness to easily launch a sneak attack. Thus, the Sandusky Indians, plus their allies, and the American volunteers watched each other across glades of tall grass and various spits of trees lit by the flickering lights of bonfires scattered around their lines, each waiting to see what the morning would bring. The British and the Indians could wait with greater confidence, knowing their Shawnee allies were on the way with the Indian agent Alexander McKee. The small guns Caldwell had left behind might even come up during the day, a welcome addition to their firepower.

During the night, fifteen men from Washington County deserted their comrades, bound eastward toward the Ohio River and home.[58]

As dawn broke around 6:00 AM on Wednesday, June 5, the British and the Indians resumed steady firing from across the open ground and tree lots that surrounded Battle Island.[59] But they did not seriously contest the American positions, instead settling on a duel among rifles at long range. Lieutenant Rose concluded at the time that the Indians simply wanted to draw American fire and pressure the volunteers to further reduce their ammunition and powder, although he later attributed the distance to having dealt the enemy "so severe a blow the preceding evening that he did not venture an attack."[60] Rose's initial impression was more accurate. Mounted men became more visible—Indians or rangers remains unclear—at different places and times around the perimeter, drawing the volunteers' attention and fire. As Rose saw it, their goals were to make the Indians appear to be present in larger numbers and invite the Americans to waste still more ammunition.[61] Simply, they mirrored some of the tactics Rose had employed during his fighting withdrawal to Battle Island.

The maneuvering, both mounted and on foot, renewed concerns about the skirt of trees Gattis had pushed the Indians from late on June 4 and the connecting wood. Williamson proposed advancing directly with 50 infantry and mounting 150 men on the best horses to flank. Williamson would command the foot troops and Rose the mounted men. Rose asserted that Crawford considered the idea with his officers and then laid it aside.[62] Rose, bitter after the battle, explained that Crawford and his officers believed the "best men" would undertake such an attack. If it failed and the attacking force was separated from Battle Island, the remainder would be unable to rescue them, endangering any hope of retreat.[63] If so, it was one of the few times Crawford was able to resist Williamson's charisma or popularity. Yet on the British side, Lieutenant Turney reported that the Americans made two attempts to sally from the island, only to be repulsed.[64] Turney does not explicitly report the timing or location of these foiled attacks, but the context from his letter suggests they occurred in the morning. Traditional accounts of the battle on the morning of June 5 accept Rose's characterization of American actions as a proposed joint attack that was dropped.

Turney's report, however, may suggest that Williamson's proposed assault on the wood line in Gattis's sector was attempted, perhaps without Crawford's endorsement, and that the lieutenant was inclined to gloss over the episode when it failed. There was visible tension between Crawford and Williamson throughout the campaign. Rose, who was supposed to act solely as an aide, consistently sought and took command of his own body of troops when the opportunity presented itself, no doubt creating resentment. The lieutenant ended up on Williamson's side of the relationship when those closest to Crawford foiled Rose's efforts to create and command a separate group of light horse. In part two of Rose's memoir, presumably composed and delivered to General Irvine in private after some reflection, his antagonism toward Crawford is palpable. For all intents and purposes, he blamed the colonel for the expedition's eventual outcome. Fixating on Crawford's mistakes during the campaign, Rose all but ignored his

own. In what is an admittedly speculative line of reasoning, it is
entirely plausible that he glossed over a failed morning attack that
he co-led on June 5.

ALL THINGS CONSIDERED, events were going well for the Sandusky
nations and the British during the morning of June 5. The long-
range exchange of fire was indeed exhausting American ammunition. Small but visible movement around the periphery of
American positions further kept them on edge and meant that a
smaller number of warriors and rangers could essentially fix an
American force in place. The warriors and rangers were free to
come and go, rest, eat, drink, and replenish powder and ball from
stores that Caldwell had brought with him.

The Americans had no such option. Indeed, John Sherrard,
who had done yeoman's service on June 4 shuttling water from
the depression made by an upturned tree, found another puddle
of water and repeated the feat on June 5, a welcome respite as
Battle Island lacked its own source of fresh water. After several
hours, the volunteer settled behind a large red-oak tree to rest,
only to fall asleep. Eventually, warriors or rangers spotted the re-
clining American and began taking shots at him, missing Sherrard but hitting the tree enough to shake loose bark that fell on
his face and woke him. Sherrard returned to his water-retrieval
mission, eventually bringing in several canteens. He had been
gone two hours and given up for dead.[65] The water was critical,
as it was proving to be another hot day. John Walters reported in
his pension declaration that the "stench of the dead and
wounded became almost intolerable."[66]

Elsewhere on the battlefield, a shot to the hip dropped one
Indian into the grass. When the Americans crawled out to take
his scalp, they instead brought back his head, a reminder that
even long-range fire and skirmishing could result in horrific sav-
agery. Deeper in the American position, men busied themselves
cooking bread and bacon or stuffing saddlebags, seemingly

preparing to depart, perhaps in a repeat of the skedaddle of the Washington County men the night before.[67]

Around noon, Alexander McKee and Simon Girty's brother, James, arrived with some Shawnee, whose number would eventually reach 140 to 150.[68] Initially they remained out of sight, but the Americans noticed an uptick in activity during the afternoon. Rose noted a growing number of visible horsemen, "which the enemy show'd us to very great advantage."[69] As the afternoon wore on, the Indians grew more daring, revealing themselves for longer periods and closer to the American lines. Taunting began, the Indians and rangers calling on the Americans to surrender and promising fair treatment. For their part, the volunteers yelled back that they were ready to have another round of fighting and declaring they would not be taken up as slaves.[70] When the Native American warriors grew bolder, some volunteers concluded they must be drunk.[71]

As the day wore on, Crawford expected an attack—which may have been why he nixed committing nearly half his force to the plan Williamson and Rose had cooked up that morning—but none materialized. Instead, late in the day, Simon Girty made his first notable appearance. Tradition has it that Girty fought with the Delaware on June 4. The next day, however, he appeared on a grey horse, riding between the lines under a white flag. He yelled out for Lieutenant Colonel Williamson to meet him between the lines, reminding us that the Sandusky Indians were still under the impression that Williamson commanded. As the second in command emerged from American lines on Battle Island, someone popped up from the tall grass and took a shot at him, missing. He quickly found a tree to get behind while the volunteers spotted several Indians moving to cut him off from the main lines. They fired at the Indians, reportedly hitting a few, as Girty turned on his horse and galloped away.[72] At least that is one version of events.

Another that originated with the Wyandot, among whom Girty was staying, has Girty approaching the lines and asking for Colonel Crawford. The two met. Girty told him he was outnumbered three to one, but there was a gap in the Indian lines to the east. By heading through that gap, Crawford and his volunteers could escape the battle and return east. Its source was allegedly Wyandot oral tradition, and whites frequently repeated it in the first half of the nineteenth century. By the last half of the 1800s, historians had dismissed it as wholly fictitious.[73] A third version has Girty riding out between the lines and calling for Crawford, riding back and forth and offering a parlay with Captain Elliott. Crawford did not respond, and eventually Girty returned to Indian lines.[74] A fourth version has Crawford and Williamson emerging from the tree line to meet Girty, only to be fired on by hidden Indians, leading some to conclude the call for parlay had been a ruse. The source for the story is Williamson's daughter. It was recorded late in her life, when attitudes toward Girty were decidedly negative and Crawford had risen to the status of a frontier martyr.[75] In all the accounts, volunteers claimed to have Girty in their sights when he rode off.

IF THE DELAWARE, Wyandot, and handful of Lake Indians who had fought Crawford and his men on June 4 grew more bold as June 5 progressed, the afternoon proved truly disheartening to the Americans. Butler's Rangers became more visible and moved along the periphery in mounted groups, leading some Americans to conclude they had just arrived.[76] Although Lieutenant Turney reported the Shawnee arrival around noon, those Indians were most likely the scouts and a respected leader or two. They would have come ahead to consult with Dunquat, Captain Elliott, and Lieutenant Turney to determine the best place for the main Shawnee body along the battle lines. On the afternoon of June 4, the Delaware had sprung their ambush to the north and then filtered around to the east and southeast, Crawford's right flank, when the lines settled around Battle Island. The burden of trying to cut the American line of retreat to the south had fallen on them. The Wyandot remained in front, to the north between the volunteers and their villages, and probably filtered around to the west, Crawford's left flank. But there were not enough warriors and rangers to complete an encirclement. Gaps through a marshy ground to the northwest existed, as did a significant break in the south and southwest. The latter became the natural place to plug in the Shawnee, and the Americans saw them moving into position in the evening. Rose wrote, "a Body of 150 Shawnoes advanced quite openly in 3 Columns on the common road in our rear, carrying a standard (red) at the head of their Centre Column." As they arrived and spread out along the left and rear of Crawford's position, firing into the grove intensified. Michael Meyers, in Captain Hoagland's company under Gattis's command, summarized the situation, "Upon the renewal of the fight, the Americans now found themselves surrounded: The Indians bullets flew lively in every direction, & the bark was knocked from the side of many a tree: one man had the breech of his gun shot away. The Indians had a large red flag, which was conspicuously exhibited. They kept the firing until after dark, yelling terribly."[77] The gap to the rear had shrunk to roughly one quarter of a mile.[78]

Rose described their positions: the Delaware and others—the others being the Lake Indians, rangers, and Wyandot who collectively outnumbered the Delaware—occupied an arc from the right rear counterclockwise across the front to nearly west of Battle Island along a road that led to the Sandusky towns. The Shawnee camped to the south.[79] Finally, as the sun set, the Indians and rangers fired off one last massed volley, a celebratory *feu de joie* meant to express supreme confidence in a victory ahead. With that, the Indians and rangers again withdrew to their camps in the distance, leaving behind scouts and bonfires to keep an eye on the Americans in the growing darkness.

AS HE HAD THROUGHOUT THE CAMPAIGN, Colonel Crawford assembled his officers and held a council. Together they made the decision to retreat. Rose offered the rationale in his initial report to General Irvine, made after the campaign: "As these succors [the arrival of the Shawnee and rangers] rendered the enemy so vastly superior to us in numbers, and as they could collect all their forces in a circuit of about fifty miles, who kept pouring in hourly from all quarters to their relief, prudence dictated a retreat."[80] Other volunteers offered additional reasons. James Paul, probably in Captain Biggs's company, feared a renewal of the battle on June 6 "as our ammunition and provisions were nearly exhausted."[81] John Sherrard, who had distinguished himself by risking life and limb retrieving water under fire, highlighted the arrival of more Indians and dwindling ammunition stocks in relating the tale to his son.[82] Dr. Knight, the surgeon detailed to the expedition by General Irvine, also explained that Indian reinforcements and increasing American losses in killed and wounded prompted the decision.[83]

The reasons for a retreat are obvious. Paul, Sherrard, Rose, and Knight all accurately summed up the situation. In truth, if the Americans, having been tracked all the way to Battle Island, ever really possessed the initiative, they lost it on June 4, when the scouts led them to the abandoned Wyandot village. The hours spent searching for the relocated villages burned almost an entire day's worth of light, followed by a short, vicious, but stalemated battle. That it occurred was in keeping with General Irvine's hopes. That it was indecisive presented a conundrum. The odds of success fell with every passing hour, but retreat meant forgoing the possibility entirely. At the same time, the difficulty and risks associated with both remaining and retreating rose with every passing hour.

Oddly, the timing of the decision to retreat is less certain. Explaining it by referring to the arrival of substantial Indian reinforcements suggests the decision was made afterward, perhaps after the sunset *feu de joie*. Indeed, John Slover, the scout, reported secondhand that in the evening, Crawford proposed the withdrawal. One of the most thorough studies of the battle argues that Crawford called a council after the *feu de joie*, in which Major Leet proposed launching a surprise attack to the west to break the Indian encirclement, take an old trail south, then circle back to an old army road. The council rejected his plan and decided on retreating down the southern road, between the Delaware and Shawnee positions. Crawford's most recent biographer endorses this evening council making the decision.[84]

But James Paul's account indicates that the retreat was to begin at six o'clock and that preparations for it, such as baking bread, took place during the day. In fact, the men used the very spade recovered at Gnadenhutten on May 28 to do exactly that. Paul later accidentally stepped on it while it was still hot, burning his foot severely before going to sleep on June 5. (His moccasin had worn clean through the bottom.)[85] Dr. Knight also identifies time-consuming work that took place between the point that a decision to retreat was made and its implementation after dark, namely building sufficient biers to carry the wounded over a long journey.[86] Rose confirmed that the orders to build biers for the wounded had been issued for the purposes of conducting a retreat. He also reported that the men began to assemble for their retreat immediately after dark, suggesting that the decision had been made during the day. (He is more circumspect about where the idea for retreat originated.) While the original plan had been to assemble by units, Rose indicated that the plan changed, and men were ordered to go individually to their horses, saddle and load them. He also reported, "A retreat was agreed on to be made in the night," suggesting that it was not yet night when the retreat was agreed on.[87] Collectively, these data points suggest a daylight council, which must have occurred before a *feu de joie* that was fired at sunset. Two early historians of the frontier, Alexander Withers and Joseph Doddridge, both take that notion as a given. They followed the local-tradition methodology, which involved collecting family stories, recollections, and available first-person accounts to record history. The approach suffers significant weaknesses, but in many cases it was all that was available among a population that may have been illiterate at the time of events. Still, Withers and Doddridge created standard histories for events in the Ohio country for decades and, in the absence of better information, need to be taken seriously, with the limitations of their methodology in mind.[88] In this case, their acceptance of a decision to retreat at an earlier, daylight council fits well with the extensive preparations noted by Rose, Knight, and Paul. The campaign's first historian, C. W. Butterfield, accepts this notion and places the council during the late afternoon or early evening, suggesting it took place close to the time the Shawnee were seen arriving.[89]

A daylight decision to retreat means the volunteers had reasonable time to prepare for the action. The plan was simple enough: bake bread for the march, prepare biers to haul the wounded who could not sit on a horse, build fires up around American lines as if preparing to camp for the night, assemble the men on their horses by unit and put them in march order in the center of the American position, quietly pull in the pickets around the periphery, then move out in two or three columns, wounded in the middle.[90] The volunteers planned to take a roundabout route. They would follow a trail used by the leftmost column during the advance and presumably west of the main road from the old Wyandot village.[91] The intended route traveled around the Shawnee camp, putting it between the volunteers and the Delaware. It was longer than the main road directly between the Shawnee and Delaware camps, but the western fringes of the battlefield held fewer warriors.

Things started well. After dark, the companies were collected and organized into their assigned places in the column, and officers departed for the outer perimeter to call in the sentinels. (It should be remembered that sentry duty was performed throughout the campaign somewhat reluctantly and haphazardly.) Not surprisingly, the march order assigned for the retreat differed from that created during the advance. Williamson's men had led the way west, but Major McLelland's right wing would lead the march out.[92]

Events, of course, rarely follow a plan perfectly. An officer under Colonel Gattis in the rear body opted to lead his men out before the order was given. "Capt. Hardin at the head of a large party, thinking our enterprize rather hazardous, was moving off toward the town first, and expected by a circuitous march to fall into our path & by that means avoid the enemy's vigilance."[93] Captain John Hardin, apparently a miller by trade, had raised his objections earlier and motivated—manipulated in Rose's view—a group of younger men by playing on fears of Indian numbers. (Hardin appears to have marched to the north and west, toward the Wyandot town and a perceived gap in the Indian lines.) Crawford ordered Rose and Major William Harrison to detain the column while he went off in search of Hardin's men, hoping to bring them back. Whether by happenstance or Hardin's decision to lead a group of men out prematurely, Indian scouts around the perimeter promptly detected the commotion on Battle Island. They began shooting, spreading an alarm all around the American positions. The result was predictable.[94] While Colonel Crawford was off doing a job more suitable to Colonel Gattis or a staff officer such as Rose or Harrison, poorly trained volunteers—exhausted from two days of skirmishing mounted on farm horses worn out from weeks of riding, low on food, short on water, powder, and shot nearly spent, confused in the darkness, and afraid of being left behind—started to panic.

Rose observed, "that instant every Body was pushing as if it had been a signal agreed on for that purpose." One of the scouts in the rear of the column, John Slover, stated it simply: "our men broke and rode off in confusion, treading down those who were on foot, and leaving the wounded men who supplicated to be taken with them." Major McLelland, who had been shot in the foot, dismounted and handed his horse over to John Orr. Moving among his men, who were expected to lead the retreat, the major struggled to restore order. Regrettably, they ignored him and rode on, leaving him behind.[95]

Any organization Crawford and his officers had attempted to impose for the retreat quickly fell apart. Rose remembered: "By a secret impulse the whole took pall-mall to the south, collecting as they kick'd along, to some one officer or other; except some few paraded in front of the Line. these thinking the Rear was pushing after them and not willing to loose the chance of getting first through—cut and whipp'd at a horrid rate along the path." As volunteer Michael Walters saw it, "the men got scattered through other and left some on the lines I believe Every one took his own road."[96] Rose fell in with a group of about fifty men who followed the intended route northwest of the Shawnee camp, but a large portion took a different trail, passing by the other side of the camp. McLelland's men barreled straight into Native American warriors alerted by the earlier firing and now "suffered considerably," as nearby Indians gathered and fired into the retreating column. Those following veered west, away from the gunfire ahead in the darkness.[97]

In Captain Biggs's company, John Sherrard, the intrepid water carrier, shook his friend, James Paul, awake with an alarmed, "Jamy, Jamy, up, and let us be off; the men are all going." Still nursing his burned foot, Paul found the sapling he had tied his horse to. Sometime while he slept, however, the horse had slipped its bridle and wandered off. Groping around in the dark, Paul discovered two other horses tied to the same sapling and his own mount standing calmly at their tails. He put on the tack, mounted up, and joined a group moving away in the darkness.[98] Clearly, not everyone had gotten the word in a timely fashion that the volunteers were withdrawing. The panic only made things worse, and groups began to scatter.

Slover, who had been at the rear of the column feeding horses when the volunteers began to break, fell well behind the main body, "which had passed by me a considerable distance before I was ready to set out." Moving swiftly up the column, he caught them before they finished crossing a glade—most likely the one over which Crawford had advanced to Rose's relief on June 4— and almost reached the front. In doing so, he separated himself from the cluster of five or six men with whom he had been feeding horses. But reaching the front of the column, he encountered his original group again and found "their horses had stuck fast in the morass, and endeavouring to pass, mine also in a short time stuck fast." Slover struggled with his horse for a time as the column continued moving away until he heard Indians approaching behind and to either side. Finally, he abandoned his mount for a faster getaway on foot and reached the other side of the boggy ground, where he rejoined his earlier group, who had done likewise. Two had lost their guns.[99] Among them was James Paul, still nursing his burnt foot. Like Slover, the group had ridden into the muck and was compelled to dismount and abandon their horses. To pick their way across, the men had to move from "tussic" to tussic of thicker grass all the way across. One poor member of the party, whom Paul described as a "little fearful man . . . who ought to have stayed home" was too short to make the leaps in a single bound. He constantly slipped into the mire up to his armpits and then had to struggle mightily to get out. His fear of being left behind was palpable.[100] Indeed, it was widespread among the volunteers.

Mike Myers in Hoagland's company under Colonel Gattis also found his way into the quagmire. As the Indians spread the alarm, warriors began rushing the American lines. Myers soon found himself beset by several warriors and laid about with a clubbed rifle. He was wounded in the hand, and the Indians forced him to the ground in a dogpile, but he managed to throw them off long enough to reach a marsh. Up to his armpits in it, he pushed around logs and brush and stumbled upon Martin Swigart, whom he knew from home. The two reached the other side, just as Sherrard had, where they encountered a third man shot in the ankle. He begged them to dig out the ball, but his screams led Myers and Swigart to abandon the attempt lest it attract Indians.[101] They left him.

On Battle Island, Francis Dunlavy, who had dueled the big Shawnee Kekewepelethy on June 4, was crouched behind a fallen log with a younger volunteer. Together they had one horse. Dunlavy was ready to leave, but his companion was too afraid. Finally, an Indian charged them. Dunlavy's courage from the day before fled in the darkness; he quickly jumped onto the horse and followed it, alone.[102]

A wounded Captain Ezekiel Rose in Williamson's advance body began reciting the Lord's Prayer. Frantic, he kept making errors and was unable to mount his horse. Major Leet finally shoved him onto it. In the moment, the major simply did what was needed in the chaos immediately around him. When Major Brenton, normally commanding the left wing of the main body, was wounded amid the night's gunfire, Leet stepped up, took command of Brenton's troops, and ordered them to charge west, through the Indian pickets. Some ninety men cleared the Indian lines and made their way home separately from the rest of the volunteers, although Leet's role in ensuing events is lost.[103]

As for Colonel Crawford, he never found Captain Hardin's men and ended up falling in with the volunteers rushing south, no longer in command of the situation. They had barely gone a quarter mile when Dr. Knight heard him calling out for Major Harrison (his son-in-law), John Crawford (his son), William Crawford (his nephew), and "major" Rose. Knight may have assumed that "major" Rose was Lieutenant John Rose, but Major William Ross commanded a company and was also one of Crawford's nephews, as was James Munn, who also commanded a company under McLelland. [104] So one should not assume that Crawford was assembling a command staff. It is equally plausible that the colonel was simply looking for family. John Crawford was among the men Leet was leading west.

Knight approached Crawford in the darkness, and the colonel recognized his voice. The doctor told the colonel he was sure the men Crawford wanted were all ahead with the larger body of troops.[105] Of course, the doctor had no way of knowing that and likely wanted Crawford to keep moving rather than pausing to look for his family members. Crawford insisted that the men he sought were not in front of him. Noting his horse was exhausted, Crawford announced he intended to continue searching and asked the doctor to remain with him, which Knight did. The colonel continued calling out as the remainder of the volunteers passed him by, but there was no response. He condemned the volunteers for riding off and leaving some of the wounded behind. He and Knight were alone briefly when two men, one old and one young, rode up. They had not seen Crawford's family members either. About this time, a hot firing broke out ahead of them, where they supposed the bulk of the volunteers were. In all likelihood, these were McLelland's men, whom Rose had noted attempting to stay on the road south and exploit the rapidly closing gap between the Delaware and Shawnee camps. Crawford and his three companions took a different route, moving southwest, probably not too far from Rose's route. At some point they turned north, most likely thinking they were behind the Indians, and stayed on that track about two miles before turning east when they felt it was safe. The four men kept fifteen or twenty yards between them, perhaps to reduce their visibility and provide some warning of an ambush. Although only four men, their journey was typical for the small bands of volunteers trying to escape the Indians who hovered on the fringes in the darkness looking for opportunities to attack.

The older man in the party often fell behind in the darkness and called out for Crawford and the rest of the party to wait for him. Near the Sandusky, he called out again. Just as Crawford, Knight, and the young man prepared to lash out and demand he keep quiet, Knight heard an Indian "halloo" roughly 150 yards away, after which they never heard from the man again. The straggler's escape was cut short around midnight on June 5.[106]

AMONG THE LARGER GROUPS, Rose's fared well. The men initially rode to the west and southwest, taking a path around the Shawnee camp and avoiding the Indians who were gathering and firing on the larger group headed down the southern road. In the darkness, however, the volunteers missed a split in the trail and ended up on a route toward the Shawnee towns rather than a more southerly direction toward the abandoned Wyandot town. They were already down the path two miles when the moonrise revealed their error. Among them was Angus McCoy, assigned to Captain Bilderback's company in McLelland's right wing, the same Major McLelland whose troops had abandoned him at the first sound of gunfire and run directly into gunfire to the south of Battle Island.[107] McCoy's presence with Rose suggests the amount of chaos that night. McCoy and his company would have been in the thick of that fight if McLelland's wing had any cohesion. McCoy described riding by the swamp that had trapped so many men. As his group made its way back to the main route south and east, he later recalled, "We marched all night as fast as the wounded could bear and circumstances permit. The Indeans did not annoy us any more that night, we supposed from our taking a wrong road or path from that intended."[108] They veered east, back toward the road they had followed north. Rose and his gaggle rejoined with Colonel Williamson and a larger group at the old Wyandot town. Together they brought the total number of volunteers in the largest group to about 250 men.[109] It was finally time to focus on getting home, rather than simply getting away.

The Americans remained disordered and retraced their route across the wide open grasslands, which brought them to their June 3 campsite by a spring. One of the volunteers, Isaac Vance, spotted a brass kettle in the underbrush. Apparently, the Indians had used it to boil sap and produce sugar in the area. The fear of the night before having passed and motivated by loot, he took the time to dismount, find a rock, and pound it flat for easier transportation across the Ohio River. Williamson, in command, used the pause to organize a line of march. One of his first orders of business was to reconstitute the body of light horse that he and Rose had advocated and Crawford or his staff officers had resisted during the advance. Rose's fixation on a unit of light horse is understandable. He stated it simply, "this was necessary as the enemy was strong in light Cavalry, which he could employ to advantage in the plains, and which we ought to oppose in the same Way."[110] The term "light horse," which the volunteers used frequently, was a somewhat nebulous concept on the frontier. Traditionally, it referred colloquially to European cavalry concepts based on dragoon or hussar cavalry units, which had their roots in the more open farmlands of central Europe. They were organized and trained to fight together on foot or mounted, which usually meant carrying a saber or other blade suitable for fighting from horseback. The American volunteers had none of these. At best, they might hope to take advantage of some increased tactical mobility on the battlefield as a semiorganized force capable of reacting to emerging threats during the retreat. Rose had argued for the creation of a light horse at the beginning of the campaign while the volunteers were deep in the woodlands, before he had even seen western Ohio's grasslands. In those woodlands, the terrain often mitigated any tactical value that a unit of light cavalry might have anticipated, as Rose pointed out in his complaints during the westward trek to the Sandusky River. This did not invalidate the idea of setting up a de facto quick reaction force from the available volunteers, but Rose's emphasis on the importance of the light horse may represent a conscious, or even subconscious, desire to elevate his own role in the campaign. This is important to remember as we consider events in the afternoon of June 6.

Despite their head start and an uncoordinated response among their adversaries, the American volunteers were eager to escape the Ohio country. Angus McCoy noted the group "continued our course as fast as our wounded could bear." In particular, they feared being caught in the open of the grassland, largely because they mistakenly thought the Indians vastly outnumbered them. According to Rose, "We proceeded with as much speed as possible through the plains, wanting to gain the Woods, fearfull of the ennemy's horse." The notion that they were severely outnumbered took hold and persisted for years. Writing in 1873, the campaign's first historian, C. W. Butterfield, concluded, "The superiority of the enemy, in numbers and equipment, was painfully evident to the borderers." That preoccupation aside, Indians sniped at the flanks and rear of the volunteer column as it retreated. One of the Americans wounded on Battle Island, Thomas Ogle, was hit again and fell from his horse, immobilized. The column moved on while he planned to play dead and then kill any Indian who came for his scalp.[111]

Separately, pursuers found a young John Hays, who had gone to war dressed simply like an Indian in a breechclout. He had gotten ahead of the main column with Angus McCoy and a handful of other men. Springing from ambush, Indians caught him. They struck him in the head with a tomahawk and ripped off half of his scalp before any aid could arrive. He survived the wound, but so much blood covered his face that some volunteers mistook him for an Indian. They nearly killed him before he could stammer out his name.[112] Behind the column, David Harbaugh had been separated from his company and straggled along with John Sherrard. After the sun rose in the early morning, they entered a copse of woods south of the old Wyandot town, with Sherrard riding well ahead. The water carrier spotted an Indian off to his left, jumped down from his horse, found cover behind a tree, and warned Harbaugh of the danger. The straggler could not spot the Indian though and ran for Sherrard, putting himself on the wrong side of the tree. The Indian shot him mortally, and Harbaugh's last utterance was the recognition of death. When the smoke cleared, Sherrard spotted the Indian running away, already well out of rifle range. The volunteer stripped Harbaugh's horse of its tack, set it loose, and turned his horse east. A half mile on, the thought of Harbaugh's provisions and blanket struck him. So he turned back. Finding Harbaugh's now-scalped body, Sherrard retrieved the man's wallet and then replaced his own worn saddle pack with Harbaugh's superior gear.[113]

As the day unfolded, exhausted men and horses began to straggle and fall out of line. Any formation Williamson had coaxed out of the volunteers at the springs slowly dissolved. Pursuing Indian warriors and rangers had already made their presence known on all sides, including in front of the massed Americans. To keep things on track and prevent small groups of men from riding off on their own, Lieutenant Rose, his servant Henry, Major Harrison, and William Crawford rode forward of the main body. (Harrison and Crawford were respectively Colonel Crawford's son-in-law and nephew.) As they were riding ahead some two hundred or three hundred yards from the largest mass of vol-

unteers, they passed a small group of trees on their left. A number
of the "enemy horse" sallied from the woods. Rose double-timed
back to the front of the volunteer group but was nearly cut off by
rangers who had almost gotten between his small group and the
volunteers. Henry also managed to dodge the rangers by riding
around a hill. Seeing the two men approach, with enemies on
their heels, the reassembled light horse in the American body
spurred forward and drove the rangers off. Rather than running
the gauntlet, however, Harrison and Crawford spurred south and
disappeared.[114] The greater number of rangers and Indians
chased them, rather than rush headlong after Rose into the main
American body.[115]

IF CHAOS DOMINATED American actions on the night of June 5-6,
things were only slightly better among the Native Americans and
British rangers beyond Battle Island. According to Lieutenant
Turney, the Americans "made their escape about 12 o'clock at
night, though some of the Indians pursued them." C. W. Butterfield argued that the Indians were confused by the American action, unsure what the volunteers intended: attack, retreat, or
some sort of feint.[116] Most of the Native American warriors, however, had withdrawn to their camps farther away, and it took time
for word to travel. After the Americans broke, the Indian warriors
pursued them in much the same way the volunteers fled: piecemeal in groups of varying size. Presumably, those with horses pursued the Americans most closely, overtaking stragglers, killing a
number, and taking a few prisoners. Despite the widespread firing
of long arms, nobody alerted the rangers until dawn. It could
have been confusion, an oversight, a decision to exploit the victory unilaterally, uncertainty about a proper course of action, or
simply the kinds of delays associated with the fog of war. Turney
quickly mounted his men and joined the Indians in pursuit. Despite beginning his pursuit after dawn, Turney, his rangers, and
some notable number of Indians were able to take a more direct

route to intercept the volunteers on their line of march. They quickly caught up and had been harassing the enemy rear and flanks all morning, killing men like David Harbaugh and taking prisoners.

The increasingly visible presence of Native American warriors and mounted rangers heightened a sense of fear among the Americans. Although their numbers were about even, the volunteers had convinced themselves a thousand or more Indians and rangers pursued them. Under such circumstances, they had fixated on the grasslands as their place of greatest vulnerability to the enemy's light horse and the woods as a place of refuge. Rose summed up their mindset: "Our men had conceived the most hideous notions of the ennemy's multitude. they all thought, if they were overtaken in the plains, particularly dreading the ennemy's cavalry, not a single Man could escape; & that this would be the ennemy's intention, was allowed by all hands officer and private."[117]

Shortly after noon, as the volunteers came within a mile or so of the woods, Williamson decided to stop at a creek. They had been moving nearly nonstop since just after sunset on June 5, with little sleep on June 3 and 4. The horses and men, some on foot, were tired, and the lieutenant colonel decided to water them. As loosely organized companies rode in, disordered and seeking a place from which to refresh, the men mixed with one another, further breaking down the rough march order established overnight. It was Turney's opportunity to do more than harass the flanks and an Indian chance to do more than pick off stragglers.[118]

When the volunteers paused to refresh the horses at Olentangy Creek, Indians and rangers attacked the rear both on foot and from horseback.[119] Reacting, volunteers at the rear returned fire. Some men began to desert. Williamson quickly rode to the scene and rallied his men, holding the attackers at close range. But rather than taking command, he led by example, taking a post behind a tree and focusing entirely on killing an Indian rather than organizing his men to fight as a unit.[120] As a result, the fighting at the rear was intense but pell-mell. Captain Joseph Bean took a round through his body. On the other side, the French interpreter LeVilliers, who had breakfasted with Johnathan Leith on the morning of June 4, demonstrated some reckless bravado by donning a flashy ruffled shirt and painting a target on his chest, proclaiming, "Here is a mark for the Virginia riflemen!" Indeed, an American bullet found him on the Olentangy, and he died on the spot.[121] At nearly the same time, Rose spotted a party of warriors, possibly with some rangers, moving around toward the front, where it might cut the volunteers off from the woods, and another group preparing to "detain us on the spot."[122] Anyone looking to the skies would have seen dark, water-laden clouds gathering.

While some Americans fled and others milled about unsure what to do, the core of American resistance was sufficient to dissuade the Indians and rangers from pressing their attacks. After about an hour, they broke off, returning to a habit of sniping at the rear and flanks of the mass of volunteers. Rose's mounted reaction force was organized well enough to push ahead into the trees, gaining way for the Americans to resume their retreat. Biggs's company, which had been holding the rear during much of the retreat, was reduced to nine men and exhausted. All of its officers were missing, and volunteer John Rogers had stepped up to assert leadership. He requested relief for the remaining men. So other companies rotated through as rear guard for the remainder of the retreat.[123]

IN RETROSPECT, Rose concluded that blind chance helped the Americans escape the skirmish and that the desertions were a positive development. Indeed, he went so far as to argue "the consequences of this affair were favourable in two respects. We got rid of all our cowards, and the enemy got a sufficient check, not to molest us any more on our march."[124] As the Indians and rangers moved off, the remainder of the volunteers entered the woods.

The skies chose that moment to open up and dump rain by the bucket load on Indian and volunteer alike. It must have been welcome to men parched after two days of fighting who had made do with small amounts of muddy water from puddles and dirty streams, but it further slowed the volunteers' moving back toward the Ohio River, soaking them to the bone. Americans continued to leave the main body, getting lost, separated, captured, or deciding to make their way home individually and in small groups.[125]

After riding through the deluge, the volunteers finally settled down to rest around six o'clock among a range of thickets. They had more wounded after the fight at Olentangy Creek, the men were drenched, and their shrinking supply of gunpowder was damp. Originally, their intention was to pause a mere two hours, during which they lit bonfires to dry themselves out and offer some comfort to their wounded. But when it came time to leave, it was impossible to find the path out of the underbrush and through the trees in the darkness. So they remained until dawn on June 7. At least two men and the wounded youth, John Hays, remained behind to bake bread. Shortly after, the scalp halloo— a high-pitched, shouted cry that the volunteers knew all too well—rang out. The three bakers never returned to the volunteer caravan struggling east. Rain still plagued the march, which made slow progress along the trail made muddier by the moment. As readily as some groups of volunteers left and other stragglers joined the plodding column, it stretched even longer along the path, never truly organized.[126] John Sherrard, plodding along the same route, finally caught up with the men around sunset. They had already made camp for the night, and he reported cheering and the musical sounds of a French march. He whistled along with the tune while reporting on Harbaugh's death and tales of his escape.[127]

The night of June 7–8 was cold enough to generate a heavy frost that settled on the few open glades the volunteers encountered. But they still made good time in daylight and crossed the original westbound track and the eighteenth-century equivalent of frontier roads improved, allowing them to make better time. Presumably having learned at least some lessons, they adjusted their route around creeks and morasses, avoiding the vulnerable defiles and crossing points that had infuriated Rose during the march west. Officers were able to form their force into some semblance of the four-column formation that Crawford had intended them to take during the march west. Throughout the day, men continued to come and go from the column, some joining it for safety, others departing, thinking they could make better time on their own or in small groups. The volunteers camped about six miles from the Muskingum, between the sites of the burned-out towns of Schoenbrunn and Gnadenhutten. After sending small reconnaissance parties to both towns, they crossed the river on June 10, counting 380 men still with the group. It rained again the next day, and more men began to break off from the column, headed for relative safety across the Ohio River. Rose left the column on June 12, bound for Mingo Bottom with his servant Henry. The job before him was to arrange river transport to help bring the wounded across the river. After a long day's ride, he arrived around 6:00 PM to find that some canoes were already there and in use. Word of the defeat had traveled to Pittsburgh, likely delivered by those who deserted on June 4. A number of people had gathered at Mingo Bottom in the expectation that some survivors from a presumed massacre would make their way home.[128]

The rest of the men arrived on June 13 and began crossing, splitting up on the other side to return to their homes just as they had assembled. Rose and Williamson composed their reports to General Irvine. Williamson's was brief, no longer than a paragraph really. It related his retreat with the largest body of men, avoiding the Shawnee camp, for the most part, then being joined by a few companies. These were likely the men with Rose. He offered little in the way of a battle narrative or explanation for the retreat; indeed, he did not admit to defeat at all and left the question of casualties ambiguous, noting "the number lost, I think, cannot be ascertained at this time." Instead, he spent more time praising Lieutenant Rose for his assistance and character and

Irvine himself for the favor he had done the campaign at the out-
set. Crawford's disappearance rated a mere postscript.[129]

Rose's report was more thorough. Although the term "spin"
was not in use at the time, his letter to Irvine presents things in
the best light, emphasizing the obstacles the expedition faced,
particularly its "small" size. While also not admitting defeat, he
attributed the lack of success to the loss of surprise and the arrival
of Shawnee reinforcements on June 5: "As these succors rendered
the enemy so vastly superior to us in numbers . . . prudence dictated a retreat." Just as Williamson had credited Rose's performance, the lieutenant concluded, "The unremitting activity of
Colonel Williamson surmounted every obstacle and difficulty, in
getting the wounded along." Crawford rated only two mentions
in Rose's report, that he was missing and his men regretted it.
Separately, Rose estimated that forty to fifty officers and men
would be found dead or missing with twenty-eight officers and
men wounded, including at least three mortally who had been
left back at Battle Island.[130] For the bulk of the volunteers, the
Crawford campaign was over.

ON THE OTHER SIDE of the ledger, the British and their Indian allies were generally satisfied with the results. Lieutenant Turney
broke contact with the Americans on June 6, after the hour-long
skirmish at Olentangy Creek. While Indians were falling on John
Hays and his fellow bread bakers and other stragglers on June 7,
Turney was back at Upper Sandusky composing his report to
Major DePeyster. After three days of fighting, Turney reported,
"I am happy in having the pleasure of acquainting you with our
success on the 4th and 5th instant." He summarized the battle
quite succinctly: the initial engagement with Rose's men, the
American retreat to a "copse of woods," the battle for a neck of
woods connecting Battle Island to a more distant tree line, the
fighting's escalation, maneuvering around the edges, the de facto
cease fire at dusk, the resumption of fighting at dawn on June 5,

the Shawnee arrival around noon, and the Americans slipping away in the darkness that night. He blamed the Indians for "some mistake" that left an escape route unguarded. In particular, he called them out for failing to notify the British of the American retreat until daybreak on June 6. Skipping the fighting at Olentangy Creek, he noted that some Indians pursued the Americans and attributed their ultimate escape—which was not yet a foregone conclusion—to the openness of the country. In other words, where Rose saw vulnerability for the Americans, Turney saw advantage. In Turney's view, which he attributed to information from American prisoners, they had killed one hundred Americans and wounded fifty. If so, the exaggerated numbers may have been the result of fevered American minds panicked at their capture and pending fates. As important, he reported rumors that George Rogers Clark was about to invade Shawnee territory to the south, a widely shared expectation. For that reason, he planned to tarry at Upper Sandusky before following his wounded commander to Lower Sandusky and awaiting developments. He simultaneously transmitted the thanks of the Wyandot, who also wanted rum and reinforcements to face the rumored American offensive from Kentucky.[131] Indian agent Alexander McKee repeated the sentiment in his own letter, also blaming the Indians for the American escape from Battle Island and raising concerns about an invasion from Kentucky.[132] As if to emphasize the point, the Mingo, Shawnee, and Delaware also composed a speech—often a long, scripted presentation—to DePeyster. They more formally thanked the major for British assistance in repelling the Americans. But rather than focusing on the recent events, they drew his attention to the long-awaited offensive from Kentucky and requested more supplies for their own defense and to counterattack.[133]

The anticipated invasion from Kentucky was important and helps explain Turney's decision to cease pursuit after the Olentangy fight on June 6. Back at Lower Sandusky, where he was recovering from his wounds early in the battle, Captain Caldwell disagreed. He blamed inattentiveness and Lieutenant Turney for the American escape from Battle Island. When the lieutenant finally joined him outside the recovery tent, Caldwell chewed him out, also angry over Turney's decision to discontinue his pursuit after Olentangy Creek. Turney held that the vulnerable point at Battle Island was on the other side of the encirclement from his camp and there was little he could do, continuing to blame the Indians for the lapse. The Delaware leader Hopocan also confided to Caldwell that the fault lay with the Native American warriors. (It is worth noting the Shawnee had taken over responsibility for that area.) Turney's defense and Hopocan's concession may have cooled the British ranger's ire somewhat, but he still hinted at his frustration in a report to DePeyster: "If I had not been so unlucky [to be wounded] I am induced to think, from the influence I have with the Indians, the enemy would not have left the place we surrounded them in."[134] That said, he elevated the American body count to 250 killed and wounded and expressed confidence that the pursuing Delaware warriors would finish off the rest of the volunteers. Then, like everyone else, he turned his attention to the predicted invasion of Shawnee territory from Kentucky and reiterated the need for material support to the Indians: ammunition, rope, supplies, tobacco, etc. Left unsaid was any recognition that Turney's decision to discontinue his pursuit at Olentangy meant the rangers were available to face just such an invasion rather than being scattered across the woods of eastern Ohio. In the end, everyone was content to blame the Indians, the Shawnee in particular, for the incompleteness of the initial victory, despite claiming that ultimate victory was inevitable.

British "spin" continued to escalate as word of the battle on the Sandusky made its way through and up the chain of command. DePeyster reported to Thomas Brown, a superintendent of Indian affairs, that 600 Americans had advanced against the Wyandot and 250 had been killed or wounded on the field of battle. Most of the remainder were expected to be killed, wounded, or captured before crossing the Ohio. By July, the lieutenant governor of Quebec, General Frederick Haldimand, reported to the governor that the American force totaled six thousand.[135] (The most widely reported estimate of American strength was about five hundred, not too far from the mark, so Haldimand most likely knew better and made a simple error.) British triumphalism and the eagerness of officers and political authorities to claim credit for the victory while blaming Native Americans for tactical errors cheated the Indians of their due—Dunquat and the Wyandot in particular—in coordinating the victory over Crawford and his forces, but British self-satisfaction would be short-lived. American prisoners, and there were many, were about to discover the price of defeat and experience the unrelenting barbarism that had characterized warfare on the frontier for decades, regardless of the race of the perpetrators or victims. Soon, those same British officers and authorities would have some explaining to do.

FOUR

Executions and Escapes

NATIVE AMERICAN WARRIORS HARASSED Williamson's hodge-podge command as it traveled across Ohio, killing stragglers or those briefly vulnerable. But the vast majority of men who managed to stay together and retreat in large groups made it home across the river. Not so for the smaller parties separated from the larger group. Chief among these was the reluctant commander of the expedition, Colonel William Crawford, and the surgeon from Fort Pitt, Dr. John Knight. We left the two, who had fallen in with another pair of volunteers, in the darkness of June 5. By midnight, the older of the two other stragglers had fallen well behind and called out for Crawford and his companions to wait. An Indian scalp cry pierced the night, and that man was never heard from again. Crawford, Knight, and their companion moved on, bound eastward.[1]

At daybreak on June 6, Crawford's and the younger man's mounts gave out, and the small party abandoned the horses. They kept going, crossing the plain still more slowly, but eventually moved into the woods, which extended farther west this far north of the main army. Around two o'clock, Crawford and the others crossed paths with Captain John Biggs and a severely wounded "Lieutenant Ashley."[2] The group, now five men including the wounded lieutenant, traveled another hour when the skies opened and drenched them in the same downpour that punctuated the fight at Olentangy Creek. Rather than pressing on through the rain, Crawford's party decided to set up camp and tend to Ashley. They stripped the bark from a few trees in an attempt to create some shelter and started a fire to dry out.[3]

Crawford's little band resumed its march on June 7 and had gone about three miles when it stumbled across a recently killed deer. Butchering enough of it to obtain meat and hide to carry it in, they continued another mile before spotting smoke ahead. Leaving Ashley behind with the young man who had joined them during the retreat's early hours, Crawford, Knight, and Biggs walked cautiously toward the fire. Concluding their own men had camped there the night before, they decided to roast the recently obtained venison and rest. Reunited with their wounded comrade and his caretaker, Crawford was about to set out again when they spotted a man approaching them from behind. Although he was reluctant to come forward, Crawford and the volunteers eventually persuaded him to join them, at which point he acknowledged killing the deer. They had stumbled onto him while he was in the process of obtaining meat. Fearing they were Indians, he fled without being spotted. Reunited with his fellow Americans and his venison, the hunter received some bread in turn, and the growing group moved on. Lieutenant Ashley rode Captain Biggs's horse, and Biggs rode Knight's.[4]

In the early afternoon, Crawford finally crossed the army's original westward track. The colonel, Captain Biggs, and Dr. Knight disagreed about its import. Biggs and the doctor wanted to stay off the road, which would draw the attention of Indian war parties. Crawford dismissed the risks. He was convinced the Indians would not pursue the retreating Americans into the forest.

Crawford's group had crossed that threshold the day before. Because he was senior, the other five members of the group deferred to his judgment. So they set off down the road, no doubt hoping to make better time than picking their way through the woods. Knight and Crawford led the way afoot. Biggs and Ashley took both horses and rode in the middle, about one hundred yards behind. The hunter and the young man with whom Crawford and Knight had retreated from Battle Island trailed in the rear.

No sooner had they traveled a mile and a half than three Indians sprang an ambush from the underbrush from just fifteen or twenty paces. Knight immediately took cover behind a large black oak and prepared to shoot, but Crawford must have recognized one of the warriors. The colonel called on Knight to hold his fire, at which point one of the three ran up and took Crawford's hand. When Crawford told Knight to put down his gun, one of the Indians rushed up to the doctor and similarly took his hand. Knight recognized the Indian, who also knew he was a doctor. They were Delaware from Wingenund's band and had likely followed him west to the Sandusky with Hopocan. In all probability they had spent the last few days trying to kill the very Americans they now held in their power. Less sanguine about the prospects of surrender, Biggs fired at the Indians but missed. The warriors holding Crawford and Knight threatened to kill Biggs and the others and insisted Crawford get them to surrender. He tried, but Biggs, Ashley, and the two younger men thought better of it and escaped.[5] Crawford and Knight were then taken to an Indian camp about a half mile away. Wingenund was in nominal charge, so their captors were likely members of the Delaware nation, although warriors from several tribes used or occupied the camp simultaneously at various points during the pursuit of the Americans.[6] Crawford and Knight were not the only prisoners who would pass through Wingenund's camp. It was Friday, June 7. By daylight the next day, the camp held eight American prisoners.

WE LEFT MICHAEL WALTERS, of John Beason's company normally assigned to the rear guard under Colonel Gattis, amid the dark chaos of June 5, believing everyone had taken their own road east. He fell in with James Collins and Christopher Colman, fellow volunteers. They made it across the plains and into the woods, traveling fifty miles by Walters's estimation, when the group decided to make its way back to the road and look for signs of pursuit or, hopefully, evidence that the Indians had given up the chase and were returning to the Sandusky. On the latter point, their hopes were initially fulfilled. Walters recorded in his journal, "we saw great sign of their going back from following our people." On that brighter note, the volunteers decided to stick to the road. It was the same mistake Crawford's party had made. Walters remembered, "there were Eight Indians waylaying the road who took the advantage of us and jumpt up on Each side of us."[7] Collins immediately took to his heels, but Walters and Colman decided to fight. Their resistance was very short, and soon they were on the run too. The Indians caught up with them and captured both men. Somewhere on the march, they also picked up a wounded American who had been separated and isolated. The three prisoners were force-marched through the woods until nightfall on June 7.[8] The next morning, the Indians separated their wounded prisoner. As often happened with captives who slowed them down, the warriors killed him and cut out his heart, no doubt taking his scalp as well. Later in the day their captors brought Walters and Colman into Wingenund's camp.[9] Walters spotted Crawford and six other American prisoners already there. However, they were not allowed to mix or speak. Walters identified the warriors who captured him as "Gibaways," likely meaning Ojibwe, commonly referred to as Ottawa or Chippewa. They were probably among the warriors who had come down from Detroit with Captain Elliott.[10]

The Ojibwe did not remain long in the Delaware camp with their prisoners, staying only a few minutes. An uncertain fate awaited Walters and Colman as they made their way back to the Sandusky, but the former detected a certain hesitancy among the warriors, who "seemed as Careful of us as possible." Making their way to Sandusky, the Indians took their prisoner into a ranger camp. Naturally, the rangers threatened the volunteers with hanging for fighting against their king, but they took no action. Instead, Walters and Colman spent the night of June 8 confined in a little hut outside of town. Walters, Colman, and their captors left before dawn the next day and made their way to "Big Sandusky," likely meaning Lower Sandusky. For the most part, the group remained well outside of town, but it went in to secure a bateau, which the party then took to Detroit. By June 18, Walters found himself a British prisoner at Fort Michilimackinac, an island fort in the straits between Lakes Michigan and Huron. Eventually, the American prisoners there were taken to Montreal, arriving on October 28.[11] Whether Walters considered the warriors' reasons for being "Careful of us as possible" he did not say. But the Ojibwe would have wanted to deliver their prisoners and receive a bounty in return. If the Americans were left with the Delaware, there was every possibility that the latter would execute them and take their scalps. The Ojibwe warriors' decisions to stay well away from the Ohio Indians raises the possibility that their prisoners might be seized without consent and suggests the depth of animosity that the Ohio Indians—Wyandot, Delaware, and Shawnee—held for the Americans.

BACK AT THE DELAWARE CAMP, it is unknown whether Crawford and his fellow prisoners caught a glimpse of Walters and Colman or even witnessed the comings and goings of the Ojibwe on June 8. That evening, however, a small Delaware war party arrived at camp with the horses and scalps of Captain Biggs and Lieutenant Ashley. Knight learned the other two men in their party had escaped. The exact unfolding of events after Walters crossed paths with Crawford is murky. Knight was still recovering when he dictated his narrative from a hospital bed. Hugh H. Brackenridge, an attorney and inveterate Indian hater with ambitions to spread American society beyond the Appalachians, took the story down and rushed it into print. Understandably, the two produced a highly biased account, although in fairness to Knight, he had just suffered horrifically and watched friends die gruesomely at the hands of Native Americans. The result is a story with chronological gaps that emphasizes the more sensational and horrific aspects of Knight's experience. Nevertheless, Brackenridge's version of Knight's narrative spread widely and was taken as gospel for nearly two centuries. In the 1980s, historian Parker Brown revisited Knight's story and sorted out the timeline based on corroborating evidence uncovered in succeeding years. What follows generally adheres to Brown's timeline. Departures or discrepancies are noted in the text or footnotes.

On Sunday, June 9, at the colonel's request, the Indians took him to see Simon Girty in Dunquat's town while the other prisoners were marched to an older Wyandot townsite. Of all the people fighting the frontier war, Girty is one of the most controversial. He was born in 1741 to an Irish fur trader for whom he was named and the former Mary Newton. Simon Sr. was killed in 1750, and Mary Girty married a farmer named John Turner in 1753. By 1755, the household had grown to five children: Thomas, Simon, James, and George Girty, and John Turner Jr.[12] The outbreak of the French and Indian War forced the family to leave its farm and "fort up" in Fort Granville on Pennsylvania's Juniata River. In 1756, a war party of Delaware Indians led by French officers besieged the post. The colonists surrendered, and the Indians forced the prisoners to carry loot from the fort to the village of Kittanning, where they tortured John Turner Sr. to death in front of his family. He was not the only prisoner killed at Kittanning. Eventually, a party of Shawnee took Mary and John Turner Jr. to Fort Duquesne and separated the oldest son, Thomas Girty, from the rest of the group. After an attack by frontier militia on Kittanning, in which Thomas may have escaped, the younger Girty boys were eventually separated. The Delaware

Indians gave, or sold, Simon to the western Seneca, who were then increasingly known as the Mingo. Likewise, James was sent to the Shawnee, and George remained with the Delaware.[13] Eventually, as the French and Indian War and Pontiac's War ended, all three Girty boys—now young men—were permitted to leave their tribes. Having spent so many years with their respective Indian nations, they held dual identities as both white and Indian. As such, they became intermediaries between the two societies and made their way as Indian traders, interpreters, and scouts, frequently working for Alexander McKee, who was also an assistant deputy agent in Britain's Indian Department.[14]

During Dunmore's War in 1774, while Crawford was leading troops for the Virginia governor, Simon Girty served as an interpreter and messenger. When the Revolution broke out in 1775, frontier loyalties were divided and uncertain, with many taking a wait-and-see approach to events in the east. Residents were more concerned with sorting out the results of Dunmore's War and competing claims from Virginia and Pennsylvania over control of Pittsburgh. The Six Nations, popularly known as the Iroquois, approached Girty to translate for them in July discussions with whomever controlled Fort Pitt. (They may have selected Girty for his skills as an interpreter and because of his ties with the Mingo.) The same month, commissioners from the Virginia Assembly approached Girty to serve as a guide and interpreter for Captain James Woods, who would serve as their messenger to the western Indian nations, most notably the Wyandot, Delaware, and Shawnee, and seek to preserve neutrality among those tribes. Their mission, more perilous than anticipated, succeeded, at least in the short term.

In the Revolution's early months, as locals struggled to sort out loyalties, both sides courted—and both sides suspected—Girty and others, like Alexander McKee, Matthew Elliott, and George Morgan, who had profited from frontier experience and connections among whites and Indians alike. Because they lived far from Detroit, the new locus of British power west of the Appalachians, men like them often performed tasks for the Continental Congress, local committees of safety, or state officials. Morgan found himself appointed Indian agent for the new Continental Congress; McKee often found himself in jail or house arrest. Girty was stuck in the middle, performing tasks for Morgan while refusing to shun McKee.[15] (Elliott was in the same position.) Morgan and Girty eventually fell out in 1776, with the former firing his interpreter and emissary. Girty, however, moved on to other things and was recruiting a company of soldiers, which he expected to command as a captain. Instead, he was given a lieutenancy, which he resigned when his men were sent to Charleston.[16]

The frontier war escalated in 1777, when British strategy changed and they began arming Indians and encouraging raids against the Americans. Brigadier General Edward Hand, the new Continental Army commander at Fort Pitt, sought to launch a campaign against Detroit to stop the raids, but manpower limitations restricted him to a feckless attempt on a rumored British supply depot at the mouth of the Cuyahoga River (modern Cleveland) in February 1778. Girty served as a guide and interpreter while Crawford, returned from the war in the east, became an adviser. The fiasco that followed resulted in the deaths of neutral Delaware Indians, leading others to dub it "The Squaw Campaign." The victims were members of Hopocan's family.[17]

Shortly after his return, Girty decided to visit Alexander McKee, under house arrest and awaiting trial. Matthew Elliott was there. Having concluded the British would win the war, the two men enlisted Girty in their plan to defect to the British. On March 28, Simon Girty, Alexander McKee, his servant John Higgins, two of McKee's slaves, McKee's cousin Robert Surphlett, and Matthew Elliott left McKee's home, bound for Detroit. James Girty, ostensibly leading a packtrain full of gifts to the Shawnee from George Morgan in an attempt to maintain the peace, changed his course as well, eventually joining his brother at Detroit.[18] Not long after, Simon Girty was leading Indian raids against American farms and villages, killing civilians or taking them captive, burning buildings and crops, and besieging forts. Among all the men who had turned their coats, Girty became the focus of American hatred and fear. Crawford, however, knew there was more to Simon Girty than the fearsome devil conjured up in frontier stories. So, it was natural for him to seek a meeting and discuss his options on June 9.

There are several versions of what passed between Girty and Crawford. They all began with Knight's account, which notes that Crawford was "very desirous to see" Girty. The former American scout informed Crawford that the Indians, particularly Hopocan, were all "enraged" at the prisoners and told the colonel that his son-in-law, Major William Harrison, and his nephew, William Crawford, had been captured by the Shawnee and pardoned. It was not true, and Girty likely knew it.[19] Finally, as Knight related it, Girty promised to do everything he could for Crawford. While they were talking, Hopocan visited the rest of the prisoners and painted all of their faces black, usually a sign of death.[20]

Knight's limited report from Crawford offers little content, but other sources provide additional detail. Over time, it became accepted that Girty told Crawford the Delaware held him responsible for the Gnadenhutten massacre. Shocked, Crawford denied it and stressed that his campaign had not resulted in any casualties among the Moravian Indians. Naturally, he wanted Girty to convince the Delaware of that truth. In the process, he reportedly promised to reward Girty financially for the effort and reveal important military secrets.[21]

Alexander McCormick was a frontier trader who managed to maintain his business in the Ohio country during the war. Girty's meeting with Crawford may have taken place in his home. In her later years, McCormick's wife, Elizabeth Turner, claimed to have witnessed the meeting. According to her, Girty suggested an escape plan that would have gotten Crawford out of the hands of the Delaware and under the protection of the British, so he might end the war as a prisoner at Detroit or some other British garrison. The escape plan also traces its heritage to the widow of Girty's son, who reported that the British Indian agent would leave one of his slaves at a rendezvous point to escort Crawford to some sort of safety if the colonel could "get loose."[22]

American historians traditionally rejected the three elements of the meeting: the offer of a reward, a promise to reveal military secrets, and the escape plan. Butterfield, in this first serious study of the campaign, characterized them as post hoc attempts by Girty himself and his descendants to create some distance between Girty and Crawford's execution. That said, Butterfield's summation of Girty's life gives away the historian's biases and defines the commonly accepted image of Girty: "No other country or age ever produced, perhaps, so brutal, depraved, and wicked a wretch as Simon Girty. He was sagacious and brave; but his sagacity and bravery only made him a greater monster of cruelty."[23]

Modern historians offering a more complex interpretation of Simon Girty have been more inclined to accept those aspects of the meeting at face value.[24] Certainly, Butterfield's biases are excessive and may have blinded him to a more thorough appreciation of Girty and the meeting. Simply, Crawford would not have sought to see Girty if he shared the American caricature. An escape plan that delivered Crawford up to the British instead of the Delaware makes sense as the only way Girty might hope to collect on a reward from Crawford while remaining faithful to his British superiors, but it would have involved some risk to his own position among the Indians. Because Crawford was reportedly unwilling to make the attempt, there was no reason for Girty to admit to it until much later in life. Whichever details one chooses to believe, the important point is that Crawford sought the meeting, it took place, and the colonel believed Girty had promised to do what he could.

DURING THE MORNING of Monday, June 10, Hopocan arrived at the old Wyandot town where the prisoners were being held. There he proceeded to paint the prisoners' faces black, a sign that they were all marked for death. When it came time to paint Knight, Hopocan told him he would go with the Shawnee to see his friends.[25] Crawford returned from his meeting with Girty shortly thereafter. Knight might not have realized it, but the Delaware chief's comment harbored more malevolence than the simple words implied. Knight's "friends" with the Shawnee had already been executed brutally.

John Slover witnessed some of the brutality inflicted on prisoners. We left the scout in the early morning darkness of June 6, just on the edge of a large swamp he had struggled across after abandoning his horse in the muck. He joined five or six other men, including James Paul with his burned foot. This group decided to head north, toward Detroit, betting that the bulk of the Indians were pursuing the main body in the opposite direction. Every step was painful for Paul, but the alternative was worse, and he pressed on. They kept going through the night until they found themselves battling a second swamp. It being too dark to continue, they waited until first light made it possible to see a way through. Still hoping to throw off any pursuit, they turned for the Shawnee towns. Around ten o'clock, Slover, Paul, and their group paused to eat. They selected a spot overgrown with tall weeds and set out small blankets. Slover dined on a small piece of pork.[26] After tearing a strip from his blanket to replace his soleless moccasin and protect his inflamed foot, Paul ate an ash cake, probably made on the same shovel that had burned his foot.[27] Unfortunately and unbeknownst to them, a warrior's path passed close by their chosen rest stop. The shortest man of the group, still covered to his armpits in drying mud, continually paced around the area, keeping his ears and eyes open for Indians. Suddenly, he dropped down and warned everyone to hide. A group of Indian warriors was approaching, and the Americans quickly scattered, leaving their scant baggage and provisions behind. Luck was with them. As they skulked in the tall grass and bushes, the Indians simply passed by without noticing them or their abandoned gear. But it was clear they were searching the area. Paul hid himself in a large cluster of low alders and reported a clear view of twenty-five mounted Indian warriors passing through in a column. As he watched, the leader paused his horse, convincing Paul that the Indians heard the Americans scattering to their respective hiding places. They cast about but eventually satisfied themselves nothing was amiss and continued on their way toward the Sandusky. At least one warrior let out a cry known by whites as a "halloo," which was answered by several more in the distance around the American group.[28]

After the Indians moved on, the volunteers returned to their rest stop, recovered their gear, and continued their trek. In the afternoon, gathering clouds finally released their contents and poured the same cold rain on Slover, Paul, and the others that was drenching the main body a few miles away at the close of the fight on Olentangy Creek. Slover described it as "the coldest I ever felt." The men hunkered down and shivered away as the storm passed, resuming their flight when it was over. The volunteers had not traveled far when they spotted more Indians ahead in the distance. These too did not detect the Americans. By nightfall, the party finally reached the woods and eventually found a spot to get some sleep.[29]

Having reached the woods and struck their original track, they could make good time to the east the next day, June 7, but the close encounters with Indian search parties set several men on edge. Slover proposed turning ninety degrees off the trail, but they decided not to on account of Paul's injured foot and another man's suffering from rheumatic swelling in his knees. The latter kept falling behind the group. By the time the volunteers crossed yet another bog, he had dropped clean out of sight. So they paused to let him catch up. Slover wrote, "Waiting for him some time we saw him coming within one hundred yards, as I sat on the body of an old tree mending my mokkisins, but taking my eye from him I saw him no more. He had not observed our tracks, but had gone a different way. We whistled on our chargers, and afterwards hallooed for him, but in vain."[30] For the laggard, it proved to be a fortunate mistake, and he arrived safely in Wheeling. For men on foot, including two with slight injuries, Slover and his group made remarkable time, and by midday they had reached the Muskingum River. (This was likely the western branch, known as the Walhonding, or one of its tributaries.) At some point they caught a fawn, which they promptly killed, butchered, cooked over an open fire, and ate at the end of the day.

Slover and his party set out at daybreak on June 8, and within a few hours encountered another party of Indians looking for American stragglers. The warriors had spotted the Americans' tracks and moved around the flanks to get ahead of the small party. Opening fire from the brush, they dropped two volunteers carrying guns. Slover immediately took cover behind a tree as the Indians called on the rest of the men to surrender, promising they would not be hurt. One stepped from cover, aiming at Slover from fifteen yards ahead. The volunteer did not shoot, fearing an Indian might then attack from behind. It was to his regret, as the warrior who demanded he surrender had fired early and had an empty weapon.[31]

James Paul, still in the group, described the brief encounter occurring in a wooded valley. Although Paul was closest to the Indians, the man on his immediate left, who was close enough to touch, was hit in the first volley. "The ball must have passed very close to me, and I supposed the Indian aimed to kill both of us with the same shot." Paul thought better of surrender and "broke and ran off at the top of my speed." But after a few yards, he turned to check behind him. In his recollection, two men were already down, tomahawked, and two fought on, presumably including Slover, who was actually in the process of surrendering. Paul took to his heels again, visibly limping. The warriors initially let him go, likely under the reasonable impression that they could track him down later at their leisure.[32]

Back at the ambush site, Slover and two others surrendered. One of Slover's captors recognized him. At eight years old, Slover had been kidnapped by a Miami raiding party, among whom he lived for six years. They later sold him to the Delaware nation, among whom he lived another six years. In 1773, he traveled to Fort Pitt with a group of Shawnee. There, some of his white relatives recognized him and convinced him to return to white society, which he did "with some reluctance." At the outbreak of the

Revolutionary War, Slover enlisted and served fifteen months, eventually marrying, becoming a father, and joining a local church. Like Simon Girty, John Slover was a man from two worlds.

The Indians retraced the Americans' steps back to a glade and recovered some horses, then set out for a mixed Shawnee-Mingo town Slover named as Wachatomakak. Slover, who acknowledged some kindness among his captors, noted their moods began to sour as they approached the town. It would serve as a way station on the route to a larger village, but that did not stop the inhabitants from coming out with clubs and tomahawks, beating the Americans as they passed by. They seized the oldest of the three prisoners, stripped him naked, and blackened him with coal and water. Slover knew what it meant: "This was the sign of being burnt."[33] The prisoner realized it portended something horrible, but the Indian warriors prohibited Slover from telling him what. Instead, the Indians, who spoke English well enough, simply assured their marked captive he was not to be hurt. Bruised and battered, the three prisoners marched on to the next, larger town. Slover recorded what happened next:

> On our coming to it, the inhabitants came out with guns, clubs, and tomahawks. We were told that we had to run to the council house, about three hundred yards. The man that was blacked was about twenty yards before us, in running the gauntlet: They made him their principal object men, women and children beating him, and those who had guns firing loads of powder on him as he ran naked, putting the muzzles of the guns to his body, shouting, hallooing, and beating their drums in the mean time.
>
> The unhappy man had reached the door of the council house, beat and wounded in a manner shocking to the sight; for having arrived before him we had it in our power to view the spectacle: it was indeed the most horrid that can be conceived: they had cut him with their tomahawks, shot his body black, burnt it into holes with loads of powder blown into him; a large wadding had made a wound in his shoulder whence the blood gushed.

Agreeable to the declaration of the enemy when he first set out he had reason to think himself secure when he reached the door of the council house. This seemed to be his hope, for coming up with great struggling and endeavour, he laid hold of the door but was pulled back and drawn away by them; finding they intended no mercy, but putting him to death he attempted several times to snatch or lay hold of some of their tomahawks, but being weak could not effect it. We saw him borne off and they were a long time beating, wounding, pursuing, and killing him.

The horror did not end there. The Indians cut the body into several pieces. They set the limbs and head on poles two hundred yards outside town. The third prisoner taken with Slover was removed from the council house, although his fate was unclear. The scout expected to be treated in the same fashion at another town. Later, Slover caught sight of the blackened, charred, and bloody bodies of three other volunteers who had been put to death the same way just a few hours before Slover arrived in town. Slover recognized two of them as Major William Harrison, William Crawford's son-in-law; and William Crawford, the colonel's nephew, who had fled in the wrong direction when they were ambushed with Lieutenant Rose and Henry on June 6. On June 9, Slover saw all three bodies being dragged outside of town and dismembered in the same way as the prisoner with whom he had arrived. Like him, their limbs and heads were stuck on poles outside of town while dogs attacked the carcasses.[34] This fate was what it would mean for Dr. Knight to see his friends, even if the doctor did not yet understand the menace in Hopocan's June 10 promise.

WHEN COLONEL CRAWFORD returned from his meeting with Girty on June 10 and rejoined Dr. Knight and nine other prisoners, Hopocan approached the American commander and painted him black as well. Telling Crawford he was "glad to see him," Hopocan also promised to have him shaved when they finally reached the Wyandot town where he might see his other friends. Thus, eleven doomed men set out on what promised to be their final days on earth. They would finally reach their intended destination for the campaign.

Along the way, the Indians separated Crawford and Knight from the other nine prisoners and placed them between Hopocan and Wingenund, marking the two as special. The others went ahead at a faster pace. After a while, Crawford and Knight began passing bodies. The Indians, presumably Delaware, had tomahawked and scalped some of those prisoners sent ahead. Finally they reached a stopping point, probably at a small village, and were reunited with the five survivors, who were kept at a distance. All were told to sit on the ground, and Knight was handed over to an Indian who would take him to the Shawnee towns, but not just yet. The Delaware had more matters to attend to. Without much warning, women and children attacked the five other prisoners with tomahawks and scalped them. An older woman decapitated John McKinley, and the group began kicking his head around on the ground. From time to time, the younger Indians paraded the scalps in front of Crawford and Knight, slapping them in their faces with the hunks of skin and hair.[35]

The rest of June 10 has become historically controversial. Knight mixed up his dates, and many of the events of June 10–11 are abbreviated or skipped entirely. Yet his version of events persisted for decades. After the morning killings, Knight reported that he and Crawford remained separated but within eyesight of each other. He witnessed a conversation between Crawford and Simon Girty but was too far away to hear its content. They eventually reached a village and were forced to run a gauntlet. Knight's recounting of the experience—both men were painted black and marked for death—was brief: "Almost every Indian we met struck us with sticks or their fists." It was less brutal than that experienced or witnessed by John Slover, but someone still hit Knight hard enough to dislocate or fracture his jaw.[36] The Delaware had other things planned for both men. Knight continued that Girty confirmed Hopocan's comments to Knight earlier in the day. The doctor's fate awaited him among the Shawnee. Afterward, their trudge to a new Indian village continued, eventually ending at Hopocan's town, which Knight mistook for the old Wyandot town.[37] In Knight's version of events, repeated for decades, the Delaware immediately proceeded to execute, or murder if one prefers, Colonel Crawford. This version of Crawford's experience became the most widely accepted version of events among Americans.[38]

However, in recent years, historians have uncovered a council meeting that places Crawford's death in a new light. In the evening of June 10, Crawford "went before a council for judgment," which Knight did not mention and may not have observed. One of Girty's recent biographers stated bluntly, "Crawford's fate was to be decided later that evening by a council of chiefs at Pipe's town."[39] In the evening, his guards brought Crawford before a growing and angry crowd. Girty served as translator. There, chiefs—presumably Hopocan and Wingenund—accused him of conducting the Gnadenhutten massacre. Crawford, of course, denied it and announced he deplored the event. It was immaterial. For the Delaware, he was an enemy and the same kind of person who had committed the massacre. In other words, his personal connection, or lack thereof, to the Gnadenhutten massacre would have no impact on the outcome. He was guilty by association.[40]

Girty at that point attempted to ransom the colonel, but that only made the British scout the target of Delaware anger. Crawford noted that he had favored the Indians killed at the Salt Licks on Mahoning Creek earlier in the war. This was the culmination of Edward Hand's 1779 Squaw Campaign, in which Crawford had advised the general, and Simon Girty had served as a scout. (It should be recalled that the victims in that campaign were members of Hopocan's family, and the Delaware at that point were disposed toward neutrality or favored the Americans.) Historian Paul Brown decided that Crawford's admission of participating in the Squaw Campaign was an act of immediate self-incrimination.[41] Indeed, Hopocan's sister, who had been present and in-

jured during the Squaw Campaign, came forward to accuse Crawford of being one of the campaign's leaders.[42] Captain Matthew
Elliott, who was reportedly present, also attempted to intercede
on Crawford's behalf, likely supporting Girty's move to ransom
the colonel.[43] With the crowd worked up, Hopocan announced
that Crawford was to be burned to death. He then told Girty that
the only way Crawford might be saved is if Girty took his place.
With that, "Girty falls silent, and judgment is passed upon Crawford—death by fire."[44]

The primary sources for this version of events are, once again,
Girty's family members later in their lives or people living with
the hostile nations around the time of the event, meaning they
were, at a minimum, tolerated by the Indians or British.[45] They
were not eyewitnesses and had reasons to rehabilitate Girty from
the American caricature. Of course, that does not invalidate the
story. A month after the event, Major DePeyster at Detroit reported to Thomas Brown, superintendent of Indian affairs, that
"every means had been tried by an Indian officer [Matthew El-
liott] present, to save his life." DePeyster went on to confirm the
connection the Delaware made between Crawford's treatment
and the Gnadenhutten massacre.[46] Of course, by that time, word
of Crawford's fate had spread across the frontier, and British officials were eager to distance themselves from the event and any
responsibility for it.

In truth, we will never know exactly how events transpired during this council meeting. Modern characterizations of it as a trial
should not lead one to believe it was a trial as an exercise in finding truth or determining guilt in any modern sense. Hopocan
had already marked Crawford for death, regardless of the
colonel's relationship to the Gnadenhutten massacre. After all,
several prisoners had already been put to death in horrific ways.
The meeting was an exercise in politics and internal tribal leadership as Hopocan maneuvered the discussion so the tribe would
confirm his decision, thereby enhancing his leadership role. It
also serves as a reminder that the Ohio Indians, and not the
British, were making the decisions in 1782.

ON TUESDAY, JUNE 11, the Delaware conducted Crawford and Knight from Hopocan's town, where the council meeting had taken place, to the banks of Tymochtee Creek, where a tall pole had been erected in an oak grove. Knight's account of what happened next is thorough and worth quoting at length:

> When we were come to the fire the colonel was stripped naked, ordered to sit down by the fire and then they beat him with sticks and their fists. Presently after I was treated in the same manner. They then tied a rope to the foot of a post about fifteen feet high, bound the colonel's hands behind his back and fastened the rope to the ligature between his wrists. The rope was long enough either for him to sit down or walk round the post once or twice and return the same way. The colonel then called to Girty and asked if they intended to burn him?— Girty answered, yes. The colonel said he would take it all patiently. Upon this capt. Pipe, a Delaware chief, made a speech to the Indians, viz. about thirty or forty men, sixty or seventy squaws and boys.
>
> When the speech was finished they all yelled a hideous and hearty assent to what had been said. The Indian men then took up their guns and shot powder into the colonel's body, from his feet as far up as his neck. I think not less than seventy loads were discharged upon his naked body. They then crowded about him, and to the best of my observation, cut off his ears: when the throng had dispersed a little I saw the blood running from both sides of his head in consequence thereof.[47]

When a musket is fired, it expels flame, smoldering wadding, and some unburned powder. Depending on the range, each shot would have penetrated or seared several inches of flesh on Crawford's body, depositing the unburned gunpowder everywhere. The next shot likely ignited at least some of the unburned powder. Thus, Crawford's body burned with every shot, both those aimed at him and from the gunpowder deposited by prior shots.

This was only the first phase of Crawford's death.

> The fire was about six or seven yards from the post to which
> the colonel was tied: it was made of small hickory poles, burnt
> quite through in the middle, each end of the poles remaining
> about six feet in length. Three or four Indians by turns would
> take up, individually, one of these burning pieces of wood and
> apply it to his naked body, already burnt black with the powder.
> These tormentors presented themselves on every side of him,
> so that which ever way he ran round the post they met him
> with the burning faggots and poles. Some of the squaws took
> broad boards upon which they would put a quantity of burning
> coals and hot embers to throw on him, so that in a short time
> he had nothing but coals of fire and hot ashes to walk upon.

Thus, burning Crawford was a communal affair. The colonel
was in enough pain to seek death as a release. According to
Knight, he spotted Girty and begged the scout to shoot him and
put him out of his misery. Girty ignored him, and Crawford called
out again. "Girty then, by way of derision, told the colonel he had
no gun, at the same time turning about to an Indian who was behind him, laughed heartily, and by all his gestures seemed de-
lighted at the horrid scene."[48]

Other interpretations are more favorable to the British scout,
with Girty declining to kill Crawford out of respect for Indian tradition and for fear of Indian retaliation.[49] According to Knight,
Girty then approached the doctor and told him he would not die
just yet but would be burned at a Shawnee town. Curiously, Girty
mentioned that some American prisoners had told him the Americans would not hurt the former American scout should he be
captured. According to Knight, Girty did not believe it and
wanted to know Knight's opinion on the matter. Of course, the
doctor was nursing an injured jaw and still stunned by what was
happening to Crawford, which he expected to experience for
himself in a few days. So he did not reply. It was a curious exchange. Paul Brown speculated that the editor of Knight's narrative inserted it later to dramatize and underscore the caricature

of Simon Girty. The possibility also exists that Knight mistook
James Girty for his brother Simon. James Girty also had a reputa-
tion for cruelty.[50] In the moment, the issue was immaterial to
Knight.

> Col. Crawford at this period of his sufferings besought the
> Almighty to have mercy on his soul, spoke very low, and bore
> his torments with the most manly fortitude. He continued in
> all the extremities of pain for an hour and three quarters or
> two hours longer, as near as I can judge, when at last being al-
> most spent, he lay down on his belly: they then scalped him
> and repeatedly threw the scalp in my face, telling me 'that was
> my great captain.'—An old squaw (whose appearance every
> way answered the ideas people entertain of the Devil) got a
> board, took a parcel of coals and ashes and laid them on his
> back and head after he had been scalped: he then raised him-
> self upon his feet and began to walk around the post: they next
> put a burning stick to him as usual, but he seemed more in-
> sensible of pain than before.[51]

The Indian into whose charge Knight had been given, a
Delaware named Tuteleu who was described as "a rough looking
man yet of an easy disposition," chose that moment to lead the
doctor away and bind him in a building at Hopocan's town.[52]
(Knight believed it was Hopocan's home.) The next day, as they
were leaving for the Shawnee town, Tuteleu directed Knight past
the place of Crawford's burning. "I saw his bones laying amongst
the remains of the fire, almost burnt to ashes, I suppose after he
was dead they had laid his body on the fire."[53] Colonel William
Crawford's campaign was over.

Someone had to live to tell the tale. A mounted Tuteleu began
Knight's journey to a similar fate at the Shawnee towns forty miles
away by driving the doctor before him on foot. Knight feigned ignorance of his fate, but the big Delaware with the "easy disposition" remained alert, scarcely taking an eye off his captive. At
night he bound his captive, which prevented him from getting
loose, and Tuteleu never closed his eyes long enough for the doc-

tor to work himself free. At daybreak, Tuteleu untied him. Gnats had descended on their campsite, so Knight offered to make a smoky fire to drive them away. It was a mistake for the Delaware. As the fire did its job on the gnats, the Delaware warrior's attention wandered. Knight saw his moment and found a dogwood stick that had burned down to about a foot and a half. Combining it with a slightly smaller stick, he managed to pick up a coal and work his way behind the Indian. Using all his might, Knight hit Tuteleu in the head, stunning him and causing him to fall face first into the fire. He managed to catch himself on his hands, burning both. While he recovered, Knight grabbed the Indian's firearm, and Tuteleu quickly ran off "howling in the most fearful manner." Knight pursued and planned to shoot him but pulled back on the hammer too hard and broke the spring.[54]

With that, the doctor gave up his chase and returned to the camp, which he quickly looted and then set out south by southeast. He walked until striking the grasslands again and lay down in a thicket waiting for nightfall. Guiding by the North Star, he crossed the plain and made it into the woods by morning and crossed the road the volunteers had followed west. Rather than repeating the mistake that led to his captivity, Knight stayed off the trail and stuck to the woods. Feeling faint and still unable to chew due to his injured jaw, Knight ate gooseberries and sucked juice from plants he thought would offer some nourishment. After three weeks of barely surviving on what he could scrounge from the forest and making his way slowly east, he was found in the woods by American hunters. Knight was so weak that they had to carry him into Fort McIntosh early on July 4. Eventually, he was taken to Fort Pitt to recuperate. Word of Crawford's fate spread quickly, and General Irvine reported it to General Washington on July 11.[55]

JOHN SLOVER STUMBLED INTO WHEELING, and his story reached Irvine's ears on July 10, just in time for Irvine to mention it in his report. The scout was able to converse with his captors in a mix of Miami, Delaware, and Shawnee dialects. Perhaps because some of them recognized him, the Indians at the Shawnee town where he was kept left Slover under a form of house arrest. He was not tied or otherwise bound but free to move around the village. The Indians interrogated him about events in the east, the status of American forces along the frontier, and so on. The news was important to the Ohio Indians, as they knew the British used information to manipulate them. Still, when Matthew Elliott and James Girty arrived in town the next day, they both denied Slover's report of American victory at Yorktown, and the Indians seemed to dismiss it. Elliott and Girty's arrival boded ill for the American. He believed Indian attitudes toward him changed with the two men in town and that Girty tried to trick him to create suspicion between Slover and his captors. Perhaps because he was deprived of his moccasins, Slover chose not to make a run for it, as the wilderness was sure to tear up his feet.[56]

The Indians held a two-week council and for some reason permitted Slover to attend, also inviting him to nightly war dances. He counted between fifty and a hundred warriors every night, sometimes more as different groups cycled through the village. Alexander McKee, who lived a few miles outside of town, visited the council on the third night, but Slover did not see him say much. It was a multitribal group. Slover saw Tawaa, Chippewa, Wyandot, Mingo, Delaware, and Shawnee warriors all coming into town. He reported that the council decided to march on Kentucky and Wheeling.[57] Slover, of course, understood the discussion. He was not permitted to attend one council and supposed it was because his fate was the subject. The woman with whom he was residing took pains to hide him that night. It may be a good thing she did. About the same time, parties of warriors brought in twelve prisoners from Kentucky. Three were burned in the village—much in the same way Slover's fellow prisoner or Colonel Crawford had been—and the other nine were dispersed to other towns, where they were reported killed in the same fashion.

The same day, Tuteleu arrived in town to announce Knight's escape. Tuteleu's scalp was cut to the bone in a four-inch wound. The Indian claimed to have been clubbed with his own musket and asserted that he had groped about for his knife, which explained cuts on his hand, and then stabbed Knight twice in the belly and back. Then he boasted that Knight was a great and strong man. Slover spoke up and informed the warriors gathered about that Knight was a frail little man, which provoked some laughter at Tuteleu's expense. The moment of levity may have passed quickly when Slover learned that Crawford had been burned to death.

Despite the danger he was in, the American scout felt reasonably safe as a prisoner. He had lived among Indians before, spoke several of their languages, and had not been seriously menaced during much of his captivity. That began to change after Tuteleu's arrival. Early the next morning, George Girty and forty warriors came to the house where he was staying, threw a rope around his neck, tied his arms behind his back, stripped him naked, and painted him black with coal and ash, much as they had marked the other prisoners for death. Girty cursed the scout, and the group led Slover to a town about five miles away. As had happened to others, on his arrival the Indians beat Slover with clubs and the handles of tomahawks and then tied him to a tree. Later in the afternoon, they took him to a partially open council house about two miles away. A post stood in the open part with piles of wood scattered about roughly four feet from the pole. The cord with which Slover's arms were tied behind him was fastened to the post, and another loop was thrown around his neck, then tied to the post four feet above his head. Thus, like Crawford, he could move about the post, but never very far. Meanwhile, the wood piles were lit and began to smoke.

Aware of what was coming and very much afraid on his trip to the site of his execution, the scout experienced a sudden calm. Slover resolved to face death with patience and without fear. Words kept recurring to him, "In peace thou shalt see God. Fear not those who can kill the body. In peace shalt thou depart."

Then Slover's salvation arrived. Where there had not been a cloud in the sky fifteen minutes earlier, strong winds blew through the area, quickly followed by a violent rain. The brief thundershower snuffed the fires, and the Indians decided to put off his burning until the next day. In the meantime, they untied him from the post, made him sit, and proceeded to dance in a circle around him, again beating, kicking, and otherwise inflicting pain on their prisoner until late in the night.

Finally, three warriors designated as guards took Slover to the equivalent of a blockhouse, where they again tied his arms behind him at the wrist and above the elbow and secured a rope around his neck that was tied to a beam. Two of the Indians quickly fell asleep, but the third stayed up asking questions and talking to the marked man. Slover waited until this third man fell asleep and began snoring. Despite having one arm numbed, Slover went to work on his bindings. The Indians roused occasionally, but no one thought to check the prisoner. He eventually freed himself just before the sun's first rays lit the sky and crept around the sleeping guards. Running through town and concealing himself in a cornfield, Slover paused long enough to remove the remaining bindings from his right arm, which was swollen and black from the loss of circulation. As the life returned to it, he made his way back to a glade where some horses grazed, threw some of his bindings over one's neck as a halter, grabbed an old rug he found on a fence, and promptly rode off, crossing the Scioto River about fifty miles from town. When the horse finally gave out, Slover dismounted and ran on, estimating that he had traveled one hundred miles from the village before stopping to take a quick nap at ten o'clock that evening. By midnight, Slover was up again and on the move. Even allowing for exaggeration, Slover understood something Crawford had not: speed was his ally in escaping pursuit.

The second thing Slover knew well was the importance of stealth. Although he followed a path at night, he left it as the sun came up and used brush to cover any tracks he left behind. Still making his way east, Slover stopped on the banks of the Muskingum's western branch that night.[58] Barefoot, he could not avoid brambles and thorns in the darkness, and the pain was bad enough for him to wait on the moon's rise before continuing. In those moments, mosquitoes plagued him. Reaching the abandoned site of Newcomer's Town, an old Delaware village on the Muskingum, Slover found some raspberries, his first sustenance since Girty had seized him several days before. Crossing the Muskingum, Slover finally paused long enough to conclude he had a good head start on pursuit, but he opted to press on without rest. On the way, he caught two small crayfish. Finally, he arrived at the Ohio River across from Wheeling, not having slept appreciably for days due to the demands of escape, flight, and the ever-present mosquitoes. At length, he persuaded a local to carry him across the river in a canoe. His escape was complete.

Slover was not the only one to make his way home after close encounters with Indian pursuit parties, but his account was recorded shortly thereafter and spread widely with Knight's. James Paul, a member of Slover's straggler group until Indians attacked and dispersed it, managed to evade capture. His injured foot precluded the headlong flight Slover had undertaken, but by hiding in hollowed-out trees and staying off trails, he managed to elude pursuit while also subsisting on berries and a blackbird he managed to catch. As with Slover and Knight, the lack of sustenance made him weak, while the mosquitoes similarly pestered and annoyed him. Still, when Paul struck the Ohio River above Wheeling, he was well enough to build a makeshift raft and cross. Eventually finding a horse, he made his way to a family fort where he found several other volunteers who had gone on the campaign. He eventually rode into Washington, Pennsylvania, where he stayed two days before setting out for home.[59]

Conclusion

"I LAMENT THE FAILURE of the former Expedition—and am particularly affected with the disastrous fate of Colo. Crawford—no other than the extremest Tortures which could be inflicted by the Savages could, I think, have been expected, by those who were unhappy eno' to fall into their Hands, especially under the present Exasperation of their Minds, for the Treatment given their Moravian friends. For this reason, no person should at this Time, suffer himself to fall alive into the Hands of the Indians."[1] So wrote George Washington when he learned of the Crawford campaign's bitter end. The commander in chief summed up the conventional wisdom about the campaign succinctly: it was a failure; Crawford's execution was revenge for the Gnadenhutten massacre; war on the frontier would hereafter be to the death.

In Detroit, Major DePeyster had a similar observation, writing Thomas Brown, the superintendent of Indian affairs, "I am sorry that the imprudence of the enemy has been the means of reviving the old savage custom of putting their prisoners to death, which, with much pains and expense, we had weaned the Indians from, in this neighborhood."[2] DePeyster's superior, Sir Frederick Haldimand, similarly tied Crawford's execution to Gnadenhutten

and hoped that by reporting the executions to Governor Guy Carleton, steps might be taken to prevent a recurrence. But he feared
they would not: "This act of cruelty is to be more regretted, as it
awakes in the Indians that barbarity to prisoners which the un-
wearied efforts of his majesty's ministers had totally extin-
guished."[3] That was not quite true and never had been, but
DePeyster and Haldimand could hardly admit it. While they
might personally deplore such brutality and rhetorically urge Indians to bring prisoners in alive, the British had awarded scalp
bounties for years and created an incentive structure for killing
prisoners. DePeyster and Haldimand's predecessor, Quebec's
Lieutenant Governor Henry Hamilton, had declared at the end
of 1777, "the rebels have furnished more blood than one could
believe existed in a body so recently formed. For neophytes, they
show themselves to be excellent martyrs . . . the Indians have done
their duty perfectly; I cannot praise them enough."[4]

THERE WAS MORE TO IT than Washington, DePeyster, or Haldimand
realized. It was not immediately clear to the settlers living on the
frontier that the campaign invalidated their approach. Williamson
and others might admit they had not succeeded in eliminating
the Indian threat from the Sandusky River, but they hardly considered their strategy or campaign an utter failure. Indeed, they
were eager to try it again and attributed the outcome to poor
preparation and leadership. With that in mind, the same local
leaders who had sought Irvine's support began lobbying him to
lead another, nearly identical, campaign. In the same letter that
communicated Crawford's fate to Washington, Irvine warned his
superior, "This account has struck the people of this country with
a strange mixture of fear and resentment. Their solicitations for
making another excursion are increasing daily, and they are actually beginning to prepare for it."[5] He was more forthcoming in
a letter to Major General Benjamin Lincoln, the new secretary of
war under the recently adopted Articles of Confederation:

That disaster has not abated the ardor or desire for revenge (as they term it) of these people. A number of the most respectable are urging me strenuously to take command of them, and add as many continental officers and soldiers as can be spared, particularly the former, as they attribute the defeat to the want of experience in their officers. They cannot, nor will not, rest under any plan on the defensive, however well executed; and think their only safety depends on the total destruction of all the Indian settlements within two hundred miles; this, it is true, they are taught by dear-bought experience.[6]

Events after the Crawford campaign seemed to confirm their strategic point: Iroquois and British forces descended the Allegheny River and destroyed Hannastown, Pennsylvania, in July. Captain Caldwell was in the field the same month, leading an invasion of Kentucky by Butler's Rangers and the Ohio Indians that besieged Bryan Station in August and culminated in the defeat of Kentucky militia forces at the Battle of Blue Licks later in the month. A second column of British Loyalists and Ohio Indians besieged Fort Henry in Wheeling in September. Clearly, a defensive posture offered little security. In other words, people living on the frontier had the right strategy but inadequate means. Not until more than a decade later, when President George Washington put Major General Anthony Wayne in charge of conducting a sustained and professional campaign against the Ohio Indians, would that shortfall be rectified.[7]

Tactically, the volunteer effort had more mixed results. On the positive side, the volunteers had mustered enough men to conduct the campaign, which was conceived and carried forward locally with no meaningful support from the Continentals at Pittsburgh or state authorities in Philadelphia or Richmond. Crawford and his men had reached the Sandusky and engaged a significant number of Indians in a sustained battle, one of Irvine's major goals. Despite its ad hoc nature, the volunteer army maintained some semblance of organizational coherence until the commencement of its retreat in the darkness on June 5. On the debit side of the ledger, the Crawford campaign was ill conceived, contingent on achieving a surprise that was a near impossibility in the Ohio country dominated by Indians. That the men pressed forward after they knew surprise was lost was a command failure. The alternative of a sustained campaign was never available. Crawford and his men also lacked a unity of purpose. Some were motivated by the promise of plunder, others by a desire for revenge, and many by the hope that driving the Indians away from the Sandusky would provide some relief for their own beleaguered homes and communities. Undoubtedly, a mix of all three goals guided many men. But Crawford failed to settle on and keep to an overriding purpose, as demonstrated by his proposal to divert to more-vulnerable Indian towns on June 1 and his toleration of Williamson's constant goading when it was evident that the original target—the Wyandot settlements—had moved and nobody could be sure where they were. Thus, American decision-making was piecemeal on June 4 and paralyzed on June 5. Crawford never put his stamp on the campaign.

A proper study of the campaign must also afford the Sandusky Indians a greater role in securing their victory. British accounts gave a disproportionate share of the credit to Major Elliott for conducting the battle, perhaps because he was the senior unwounded British officer in the field at its end. But Elliott never really commanded any Indians; he was there in an advisory capacity and, even then, had the most influence over the Lake Indians who had come down from Detroit with him. American accounts also afforded Elliott a leadership role or attributed their defeat to the machinations of Simon Girty, likely due to his notoriety and later demonization. The senior Native American leader on the field, however, was the Wyandot Chief Dunquat. He led the largest Indian faction. Hopocan, Wingenund, and the Delaware might have played more visible roles, in part due to their role in Crawford's execution, but they were relatively recent arrivals in the Wyandot territory. The settlers were bound for the Wyandot towns, and Dunquat knew the security of his nation was at stake. He was not about to place that in the hands of recent arrivals from Detroit or Delaware motivated primarily by revenge.

But because the British had not arrived when he made the most important decision—to stand and fight—he did not receive proper recognition. That he, the wider tribe, and the Delaware made that decision before the battle without the guarantee of immediate meaningful British or Shawnee support should indicate his importance in determining the battle's outcome. It is unfortunate that British and American observers and historians did not recognize this at the time.

The battle on the Sandusky also represents a major step in the formation of a western Indian confederacy. British officers and groups of rangers had worked with multitribal coalitions in battle before, but usually in raids that involved limited risk to the participating tribes. Earlier in the Revolutionary War, only George Rogers Clark had mounted serious offensives into the Ohio country—limited campaigns by Generals Hand and McIntosh, and Colonel Brodhead notwithstanding—and none had penetrated as far north and west as the Sandusky. The 1782 threat posed to the Wyandot by the volunteers forced the Ohio nations to unify in defense of their immediate homes—a unity that was quickly reoriented to the south in defense of the Shawnee. The higher stakes demanded greater cooperation, and the Ohio Indians proved they were equal to the challenge. It was a solid precedent for resisting the Americans after the war without the same degree of British support.

The Crawford campaign faded from national consciousness quickly, remembered after a time almost solely due to Knight's eyewitness account of Crawford's death, which remained in circulation as an anti-Indian tract for decades. That it had the added benefit of being mostly true made it all the more powerful. A poem titled "Crawford's Defeat" circulated on the frontier for a few decades, morphing over time as it was repeated and sung to popular melodies, but does not appear to have spread nationally.[8] Yet the persistence of Crawford's personal story dominated public memory of the campaign, driving the experiences of its volunteers and the perspectives of the Native Americans deep into the background until they became all but unrecognizable.

The Crawford campaign does not rank high in the annals of American military history. Anticlimactic defeats rarely are celebrated, especially in young countries still trying to create a national identity. Crawford lacked the charisma of George Rogers Clark, and Williamson's role in the Gnadenhutten massacre blackened his name in history. The romance and admiration that attached themselves to the Mohawk leader Joseph Brant or, later, the Shawnee chief Tecumseh never found a home with Dunquat or Hopocan. But the battle on the Sandusky represents the way Americans and Indians living on the frontier attempted to conduct the military component of the American Revolution. Ad hoc armies assembled voluntarily for combat, bringing their own equipment and conducting operations without the benefit of professional military leaders. They were amateurs and always would be. Unaccustomed to operating as large groups—which Crawford's volunteer army and Dunquat's multinational alliance definitely were on the scale of frontier warfare—improvisation in ends and means was the order of the day. As a result, roles and responsibilities were rarely settled. Thus, the continual argument over forming a body of light horse among the Americans, Williamson's hyperfocus on the object immediately before him, and the panic on the night of June 5 were predictable. Native American failures to close the gaps between various tribes surrounding the Americans and delays in notifying Lieutenant Turney of their retreat were the result of similar challenges.

Finally, Native Americans and those rebelling against the Crown both fought for their homes and the security of their families. Abstract concepts like liberty and independence were well and good but less immediate or relevant to the security challenges both sides faced on the frontier. Even notions of land ownership were not at stake. Those larger issues came later. Bigger battles and larger-than-life personalities would dominate those stories, but the Crawford campaign presaged the way forward for American and Native American alike.

Notes

INTRODUCTION: WAR FROM THE BOTTOM UP
1. Parker N. Brown, "The Search for the Colonel William Crawford Burn Site: An Investigative Report," *Western Pennsylvania Historical Magazine* 68, no. 1 (January 1985): 66.

CHAPTER 1: WAR ON THE UPPER OHIO
1. Boyd Crumrine, ed., *History of Washington County, Pennsylvania, with Biographical Sketches of Many of Its Pioneers and Prominent Men* (Philadelphia: L. H. Everts, 1882), 108.
2. Williamson, of Washington County, PA, was lieutenant colonel, 3rd Battalion, Pennsylvania Militia. Pennsylvania Historical and Museum Commission, accessed December 5, 2022, https://www.phmc.pa.gov/Archives/Research-Online/Pages/Revolutionary-War-Militia-Washington.aspx.
3. Crumrine, *History of Washington County*, 107; Franklin Ellis, ed., *History of Fayette County, Pennsylvania with Biographical Sketches of Many of its Pioneers and Prominent Men* (Philadelphia: L. H. Everts, 1882), 91.
4. Irvine to Washington, April 20, 1782, in *Washington-Irvine Correspondence: The Official Letters Which Passed Between Washington and Brig.-Gen. William Irvine and Between Irvine and Others Concerning Military Affairs in the West from 1781 to 1783,* ed. C. W. Butterfield (Madison, WI: David Atwood, 1882), 99-102. Irvine reported the deaths of two Indians who held commissions as captains. Butterfield identified one of the victims as an Indian whites referred to as "Captain Wilson," per an old history and a note from Irvine's predecessor, Colonel Daniel Brodhead, that the colonel had given him a horse as a reward for faithful service. Ibid., 102-103n1. "Captain Wilson" apparently acted primarily as a scout, and the rank may have been more of a popular honorific than a reality, which Irvine might not have understood or simply glossed over to dramatize local actions. The identity of the second Indian remains elusive. Butterfield did not believe that the men who attacked Indians at Killbuck's Island had participated in the

Gnadenhutten raid. Crumrine, *History of Washington County*, 108; James Wimer, *Events in Indian History* (Lancaster: G. Hills, 1841), 279-280. John Killbuck Jr. was the name whites gave to the Delaware Indian Gelelemend, who led a peace faction of his nation to Fort Pitt after the Delaware split openly into pro-British and pro-American camps. Whites and Indians on the frontiers often had multiple names and generally accepted those names as legitimate. Gelelemend received a captain's commission in the Continental Army and was a staunch defender of the Moravian Church's activities among the Delaware. He was eventually baptized as William Henry and died in 1811. Killbuck's Island has since disappeared.

5. Irvine to Washington, April 20, 1782, *Washington-Irvine Correspondence*, 102; Crumrine, *History of Washington County*, 108.

6. Eric Sterner, "The Siege of Fort Laurens, 1778-1779," *Journal of the American Revolution*, December 17, 2019, accessed January 6, 2023, https://allthingsliberty.com/2019/12/the-siege-of-fort-laurens-1778-1779/.

7. Wills De Hass, *History of the Early Settlement and Indian Wars of Western Virginia* (Wheeling, VA: H. Hoblitzell, 1851), 179-180; Joseph Doddridge, *Notes on the Settlement and Indian Wars of the Western Parts of Virginia and Pennsylvania from 1763 to 1783* (Pittsburgh: John S. Ritenour and Wm. T. Lindsey, 1912), 224. This is the third printing of a collection of articles initially printed in the *Wellsburg (VA) Gazette* in 1824.

8. Irvine to Washington, December 2, 1781, *Washington-Irvine Correspondence*, 75. Emphasis in original.

9. Irvine to Washington, April 20, 1782, ibid., 103n1.

10. Irvine to Washington, February 7, 1782, ibid., 89-90.

11. Congressional Resolution, September 24, 1781, in *Washington-Irvine Correspondence*, 72n1.

12. Irvine to Washington, April 20, 1782, *Washington-Irvine Correspondence*, 104-105n1. Butterfield reprinted Irvine's notes from the conference.

13. Ibid. Irvine wrote Virginia Governor Benjamin Harrison complaining of the situation and urged the governor to resolve the boundary dispute. Irvine to Harrison, April 20, 1782, ibid., 266-267.

14. Irvine to Marshel, March 29, 1782, ibid., 282-283.

15. Quoted in Crumrine, *History of Washington County*, 108. Williamson expected to be compensated for the flour he advanced. Marshel to Irvine, April 4, 1782, *Washington-Irvine Correspondence*, 286. Williamson also reportedly offered to supply some gunpowder. De Hass, *History of the Early Settlement*, 189.

16. Marshel to Irvine, April 2, 1782, *Washington-Irvine Correspondence*, 283. The Marshel-Irvine correspondence is fascinating in its own right. Irvine was hesitant in early April to supply the volunteers with ammunition and salt for the proposed Sandusky campaign. Marshel's complaint that he lacked supplies to garrison the frontier and had, in fact, abandoned one post on the Ohio even as he indicated Williamson had flour suggests that the Washington County officer may have been leveraging Irvine to support the campaign.

17. Irvine to Washington, April 20, 1782, ibid., 107.

18. Crumrine, *History of Washington County*, 113.

19. Irvine to Washington, May 21, 1782, *Washington-Irvine Correspondence*, 113.

20. Alexander Scott Withers, *Chronicles of Border Warfare, or a History of the Settlement by Whites of North Western Virginia, and of the Indian Wars and Massacres in that Section of the State*, ed. Reuben Gold Thwaites (Cincinnati: Stewart & Kidd, 1912, new edition), 328; *Narratives of a Late Expedition against the Indians; With An Account of the Barbarous Execution of Col. Crawford; and The Wonderful Escape of Dr. Knight and John Slover from Captivity, in 1782* (Philadelphia: Frances Bailey, 1783), 4. Dr. Johnathan Knight was a surgeon with the 7th Virginia, commanded by Colonel Gibson and posted at Fort Pitt at the time. This slim volume was rushed into print right after the expedition, and its title page mistakenly indicates it was printed in 1773. It was calculated, in part, to stir up animosities against the Ohio tribes. Because it contains two first-hand narratives, it will be referred to as either Knight's narrative or Slover's narrative. Knight will be discussed in more depth later in the text, but he refers to Marshel and Williamson as the best known advocates for the Sandusky campaign. Edgar W. Hassler, *Old Westmoreland: A History of Western Pennsylvania during the Revolution* (Pittsburgh: J. R. Weldin, 1900), 164.

21. Samuel J. Newland, *The Pennsylvania Militia: Defending the Commonwealth and the Nation 1669–1870* (Annville: Commonwealth of Pennsylvania, Department of Military and Veterans Affairs, 2002), 135.

22. See William A. Pencak and Christian B. Keller, "Pennsylvania in the French and Indian Wars, 1748–1766," in *Pennsylvania: A Military History*, ed. William A. Pencak, Christian B. Keller, and Barbara A. Gannon (Yardley, PA: Westholme, 2016), 19-54.

23. Joseph Seymour, *The Pennsylvania Associators, 1747-1777* (Yardley, PA: Westholme, 2012).

24. Newland, *Pennsylvania Militia*, 132-133.

25. Thomas Verenna, "Explaining Pennsylvania's Militia," *Journal of the American Revolution,* June 17, 2014, accessed April 13, 2021, https://allthingsliberty.com/2014/06/explaining-pennsylvanias-militia/.

26. C. W. Butterfield, *An Historical Account of the Expedition against Sandusky under Col. William Crawford in 1782* (Cincinnati: Robert Clarke, 1873), 24. Marshel actually managed to reinforce Fort Henry just the same.

27. Irvine to Washington, April 20, 1782, *Washington-Irvine Correspondence*, 99. Irvine also described the Gnadenhutten attackers as "country people" to his wife, differentiating them from a militia class called up for military service. Irvine to his wife, April 12, 1782, *Washington-Irvine Correspondence*, 343.

28. Doddridge, *Notes*, 206. As a young boy, Doddridge listened to the stories and recollections of those living in the area during the American Revolution, so much of his material is based on local tradition. Withers, *Chronicles*, 327. Withers worked in the same tradition as Doddridge, although slightly later. Withers first published a version of his *Chronicles* in 1831. Subsequent printings benefitted significantly from the dedicated work of Lyman Draper and then Reuben Gold Thwaites, who established one of the most comprehensive archives of material about the early American frontier. Thwaites's last edition was published in 1895, and this is the fourth printing. Although the works by Doddridge and Withers

suffered from the limitations of their methodology, which subsequent editors could only partially address, Doddridge's *Notes* and Withers's *Chronicles* set the tone for many subsequent histories. Although my citations come from the edited editions, I will refer to them by their original authors. See also De Hass, *History of the Early Settlement*, 189.

29. Butterfield, *Historical Account*, 70-72n1.

30. George Gibson to Irvine, February 5, 1782, *Washington-Irvine Correspondence*, 353-356.

31. Doddridge, *Notes*, 206.

32. Glenn F. Williams, *Year of the Hangman: George Washington's Campaign against the Iroquois* (Yardley, PA: Westholme, 2005), 191-193.

33. To George Washington from Colonel Daniel Brodhead, 31 July 1779–4 August 1779, *Founders Online*, National Archives, https://founders.archives.gov/documents/Washington/03-21-02-0599.

34. Moore to Irvine, December 17, 1781, *Washington-Irvine Correspondence*, 233.

35. Doddridge, *Notes*, 206; Withers, *Chronicles*, 327; De Hass, *History of the Early Settlement*, 189.

36. Irvine to Washington, December 2, 1782, *Washington-Irvine Correspondence*, 79.

37. Washington to Irvine, March 8, 1782, *Washington-Irvine Correspondence*, 94-95.

38. Irvine to Washington, April 20, 1782, *Washington-Irvine Correspondence*, 109. Also Irvine to Governor Benjamin Harrison, April 20, 1782, appendix H, and Irvine to William Moore, May 9, 1782, appendix G, both in *Washington-Irvine Correspondence*. De Hass, *History of the Early Settlement*, 189.

39. Irvine to Washington, April 20, 1782, *Washington-Irvine Correspondence*, 109.

40. Col. Daniel Brodhead to Col. David Shepherd, October 10, 1779, Louise Phelps Kellogg, ed., *Frontier Retreat on the Upper Ohio, 1779–1781*, Draper Series, vol. 5 (Madison: State Historical Society of Wisconsin, 1917), 97.

41. Butterfield found no evidence of a connection between those advocating emigration and those advocating the Sandusky campaign, but Irvine had no way of knowing that, and his suspicions were still front of mind. Moore to Irvine, December 17, 1781, *Washington-Irvine Correspondence*, 233. In hindsight, the connection between the campaign and mass emigration is tenuous at best, correlation rather than causation.

42. Irvine to Washington, February 7, 1782, *Washington-Irvine Correspondence*, 92. See also Col. Alexander Lowrey's opinion in George Gibson to Irvine, February 5, 1782, appendix M, *Washington-Irvine Correspondence*.

43. Irvine to Washington, February 7, 1782, *Washington-Irvine Correspondence*, 90-91. American and British officers often referred to Ottawa or Chippewa Indians in discussing the Odawa or Ojibwe Nations. In this case, Irvine uses "Ottawa" to describe the Indians. In general, throughout this book I use references in the original source material. If more than one of those names is used by the same author, there may be instances of double counting.

44. Irvine to Washington, February 7, 1782, *Washington-Irvine Correspondence*, 92. See also Col. Alexander Lowrey's opinion in George Gibson to Irvine, February 5, 1782, appendix M, *Washington-Irvine Correspondence*, 353-354. Irvine's original inquiries were made with an eye toward attacking Detroit when he might still

need to build a road capable of supporting wagons from Sandusky to Detroit. Lowrey's opinion was that this would not be practical until August due to conditions on the ground. As Irvine's thinking evolved, the need to build a road was less important, but the need for speed became a higher priority. So Lowrey's judgment was still relevant.

45. Irvine to Washington, May 21, 1782, *Washington-Irvine Correspondence*, 118.

46. Ibid. Irvine wrote his wife, "I had some intention last week to go with a party of volunteer militia against an Indian town but have now given up thoughts of it." Irvine to his Wife, May 21, 1782, *Washington-Irvine Correspondence*, 348.

47. Irvine's Instructions, May 14, 1782, *Washington-Irvine Correspondence*, 118-119n1. Colonel Marshel specifically requested a set of command instructions. Marshel to Irvine, May 1, 1782, *Washington-Irvine Correspondence*, 287.

48. Irvine's Instructions, May 14, 1782, 118-119n1.

49. Verenna, "Explaining Pennsylvania's Militia."

50. "Irvine's Instructions, May 14, 1782," *Washington-Irvine Correspondence*, 118-119n1.

51. Ibid.

52. Ibid.

53. Irvine to Washington, May 21, 1782, *Washington-Irvine Correspondence*, 113-114.

54. Butterfield, *Historical Account*, 59; Knight, *Narrative*, 4. It was also common practice to retain or sell off any plunder and distribute the financial reward to participants and local claimants, much in the way privateers at sea did.

55. "Irvine to Washington, May 21, 1782," *Washington-Irvine Correspondence*, 114-115.

56. Ibid., n1. C. W. Butterfield, ed., "Biographical Sketch of William Crawford," in *The Washington-Crawford Letters, Being the Correspondence of George Washington and William Crawford, from 1767 to 1781, Concerning Western Lands* (Cincinnati: Robert Clarke, 1877), vii-xi; Robert N. Thompson, *Disaster on the Sandusky: The Life of Colonel William Crawford* (Staunton, VA: American History Press, 2017), Kindle. Chapters 1-5 deal with this portion of Crawford's life.

57. Washington to Crawford, September 21, 1767, *Washington-Crawford Letters*, 1-5.

58. George Washington to George Croghan, November 24, 1770, *Founders Online*, accessed April 30, 2021, https://founders.archives.gov/documents/Washington/02-08-02-0270.

59. Irvine to Washington, May 21, 1782, *Washington-Irvine Correspondence*, 114-115n1.

60. Such arrangements were common in the eighteenth century and did not come with the same patina of unethical behavior they do today. But the conflicting interests may have affected how Crawford's neighbors viewed him as identities became more established.

61. Glenn F. Williams, *Dunmore' War: The Last Conflict of America's Colonial Era* (Yardley, PA: Westholme, 2017), 32-34.

62. Crawford to John Penn, April 8, 1774, *Washington-Crawford Letters*, 42-46.

63. Crawford to Washington, May 8, 1773, *Washington-Crawford Letters*, 46-49. In this letter, Crawford clearly describes the conflict as "the contradiction between us and the Pennsylvanians."

64. Williams, *Dunmore's War*, 183.

65. James Corbett David, *Dunmore's New World: The Extraordinary Life of a Royal Governor in Revolutionary America* (Charlottesville: University of Virginia Press, 2013), loc. 1849-1864 of 6724, Kindle.

66. Williams, *Dunmore's War*, 255-256.

67. Thompson, *Disaster on the Sandusky*, loc. 1888-1904 of 6229.

68. After the war, Dunmore appointed Crawford as justice of the peace for Oyer and Terminer in Augusta County, Virginia. Butterfield, "Biographical Sketch of William Crawford," *Washington-Crawford Letters*, ix.

69. Ibid., vii. See Allen W. Scholl, *The Brothers Crawford: Colonel William, 1722–1782 and Valentine Jr., 1724–1777*, vol. 1 (Berwyn Heights, MD: Heritage Books, 2016), 44; Thompson, *Disaster on the Sandusky*, loc. 169 of 6229.

70. Thompson, *Disaster on the Sandusky*, loc. 2041.

71. Ibid., loc. 2290-2305.

72. Ibid., loc. 2400; Butterfield, "Biographical Sketch of William Crawford," *Washington-Crawford Letters*, x.

73. For a quick summary of these campaigns, see Thomas L. Pieper and James B. Gibney, *Fort Laurens, 1778–1779: The Revolutionary War in Ohio* (Kent, OH: Kent State University Press, 1976); Eric Sterner, "General Edward Hand: The Squaw Campaign," *Emerging Revolutionary War Era* (blog), March 9, 2018, accessed December 22, 2022, https://emergingrevolutionarywar.org/2018/03/09/general-edward-hand-the-squaw-campaign/; Eric Sterner, "The Siege of Fort Laurens, 1778–1779," *Journal of the American Revolution*, December 17, 2019, accessed May 5, 2021, https://allthingsliberty.com/2019/12/the-siege-of-fort-laurens-1778-1779/.

74. Butterfield, "Biographical Sketch of William Crawford," *Washington-Crawford Letters*, x.

75. Crawford to Washington, July 12, 1779, *Washington-Crawford Letters*, 71-73.

76. Crawford to Washington, May 23, 1781, *Washington-Crawford Letters*, 75. Clark actually intended to attack Detroit in cooperation with Colonel Brodhead advancing from Fort Pitt. Colonel Archibald Lochry of the Westmorland County militia was on his way to reinforce Clark's force when his group was ambushed on the Ohio River in August 1781. A council finally overruled Clark, while Brodhead's efforts to mobilize troops around Fort Pitt came to naught. Lochry had been well respected and his men invaluable. Their loss later affected the county's ability to respond to Irvine's April 1782 attempt to draw on militia for the frontier's defense.

77. Knight, *Narrative*, 4.

78. Colonel William Crawford to Irvine, May 20, 1782, *Washington-Irvine Correspondence*, 363.

79. Butterfield, *Historical Account*, 119. Also, Irvine to Washington, May 21, 1782, *Washington-Irvine Correspondence*, 113-120.

80. Butterfield, *Historical Account*, 63.

81. Colonel William Crawford to Irvine, May 20, 1782, *Washington-Irvine Correspondence*, 363; Thompson, *Disaster on the Sandusky*, loc. 3096.

82. Lt. John Rose to Irvine, Friday, May 24, 1782, *Washington-Irvine Correspondence*, 364-365.

83. John Rose, "Journal of a Volunteer Expedition to Sandusky, Part 1," ed. William L. Stone, *Pennsylvania Magazine of History and Biography* 18, no. 2 (1894): 137; Knight, *Narrative*, 5; Butterfield, *Historical Account*, 77.

84. Marshel to Irvine, May 11, 1782, *Washington-Irvine Correspondence*, 288-289. Rose reported that Marshel came within three or four votes of being elected third in command and was nearly as popular as Williamson, which may also have influenced his ability to swing the election in Crawford's direction. Lieut. Rose to Irvine, May 24, 1782, *Washington-Irvine Correspondence*, 364.

85. Marshel to Irvine, May 29, 1782, *Washington-Irvine Correspondence*, 289.

86. Lieut. John Rose to Irvine, Friday, May 24, 1782, *Washington-Irvine Correspondence*, 364-365.

87. Rose, "Journal, Part 1," 137; Butterfield, *Historical Account*, 77. Butterfield spells Gattis's last name with two "d's." Major Brenton is also referred to as Major Brinton in some accounts. Leet, on the other hand, disappears from a few accounts.

88. Marshel to Irvine, May 29, 1782, *Washington-Irvine Correspondence*, 290.

89. Cook to Irvine, May 26, 1722, *Washington-Irvine Correspondence*, 325.

90. Rose, "Journal, Part 1," 137.

91. Butterfield, *Historical Account*, 126-128; William Henry Egle, ed., "State of the Account of the Sub-Lieutenants of Washington County," *Pennsylvania Archives*, 3rd ser., vol. 7 (Harrisburg, PA: Secretary of the Commonwealth, printed by Clarence M. Busch, 1896), 140. The pay came from Washington County militia funds, not General Irvine.

92. John Rose, "Journal of a Volunteer Expedition to Sandusky, Part 2," ed. William L. Stone, *Pennsylvania Magazine of History and Biography* 18, no. 3 (1894): 293-294.

93. Butterfield, *Historical Account*, 124.

94. Rose, "Journal, Part 2," 294.

95. Ibid., 293-294.

96. Butterfield, *Historical Account*, 125. See also, Parker B. Brown, "The Battle of Sandusky: June 4–6, 1782," *Western Pennsylvania Historical Magazine* 65, no. 2 (April 1982): 125n27.

97. Rose, "Journal, Part 2," 294. Rose referred to officers by the first letter of their last names only. I am connecting those characterizations to the specific officers because they line up with prominent leaders on the campaign, particularly given their roles later in this narrative.

98. Rose, "Journal, Part 1," 131-137. The biographical sketch attached to Rose's journal was originally written by William Stone for *Galaxy Magazine* in the nineteenth century. See also *Washington-Irvine Correspondence*, 117n1. Rose was more circumspect during the Revolution and did not relate his story to General Irvine and his descendants until well after the war, when he had returned to Russia.

CHAPTER 2: THE ADVANCE
1. Larry Nelson, *A Man of Distinction among Them: Alexander McKee and the Ohio Country Frontier, 1754–1799* (Kent, OH: Kent State University Press, 1999), loc. 2390, Kindle; Phillip W. Hoffman, *Simon Girty: Turncoat Hero* (Franklin, TN: Flying Camp Press, 2008), 160-161.

2. Alan Fitzpatrick, *Wilderness War on the Ohio,* new rev. 2nd ed. (Benwood, WV: Fort Henry Publications, 2005), 457-458.

3. Ibid., 461. Powell believed the American expedition was aimed at Detroit and may have conflated it with an expected attack by Virginia Brigadier George Rogers Clark, who had long sought to coordinate an attack on Detroit from the directions of Kentucky and Pittsburgh. Clark's anticipated campaign to Detroit preoccupied British leaders, as no American had achieved his level of success north of the Ohio.

4. "From Major Depeyster, Unaddressed, 14th May, 1782," *Collections and Researches Made by the Pioneer and Historical Society of the State of Michigan,* vol. 10 (Lansing, MI: Thorp & Godfrey, State Printers and Binders, 1888), 574-575.

5. "Indian Council," ibid., 576.

6. Ibid., 576-578.

7. Ibid., 577.

8. Ibid.

9. Consul Willshire Butterfield, *History of the Girtys: Being a Concise Account of the Girty Brothers* (Cincinnati: Robert Clarke, 1890; repr. Columbus, OH: Long's College Book Co., 1950), 163; Fitzpatrick, *Wilderness War,* 469. Butterfield and Fitzpatrick both report that Caldwell left Detroit with two carriageless guns. Some Americans later reported hearing cannon shot on the morning of June 4 but did not report being fired on by any artillery, while Fitzpatrick reported that Caldwell opted to leave the two pieces he had at Lower Sandusky.

10. Fitzpatrick, *Wilderness War,* 462.

11. Entries for John Butler and Butler's Rangers in Mark Boatner III, *Encyclopedia of the American Revolution,* 3rd ed. (Mechanicsburg, PA: Stackpole Books, 1994), 149, 153.

12. Thomas B. Allen, *Tories: Fighting for the King in America's First Civil War* (New York: Harper, 2010), 252-275.

13. "Butler's Rangers Dates of Officers' Commissions," n.d., originally in Great Britain, Public Record Office, War Office, class 28, vol. 4, 15, *On-Line Institute for Advanced Loyalist Studies,* accessed January 12, 2023, http://www.royalprovincial.com/military/rhist/brang/broff1.htm. Todd Braisted operates this site, which is the most comprehensive database of digital material on Loyalists and Tories in the colonies during the American Revolution.

14. For interesting accounts of Butler's Rangers and their wartime activities, see *Butler's Rangers: Three Accounts of the American War of Independence: The Story of Butler's Rangers and the Settlement of Niagara by Ernest Cruikshank; The Story of Cherry Valley by Henry U. Swinnerton; Wyoming Valley a Sketch of Its Early Annals by Isaac A. Chapman* (Np: Oakpast, 2011).

15. Captain William Caldwell, of the Rangers, to DePeyster, June 11, 1782, *Washington-Irvine Correspondence,* 370-371; Nelson, *Man of Distinction,* loc. 2399.

16. Fitzpatrick, *Wilderness War,* 463.

17. The Five Nations eventually numbered six, and whites typically referred to the grouping as the Iroquois Confederacy. The word "Haudenosaunee" is more accurate, but for the reader's ease I refer to that grouping as the Six Nations or the Iroquois. Of course, other Indian nations lived in the region and played a role in the conflict.

18. Daniel K. Richter, *Before the Revolution: America's Ancient Past* (Cambridge, MA: Harvard University Press, 2011), loc. 1817 of 6313, Kindle. The seventeenth-century period of conflict is sometimes referred to as the Beaver Wars, somewhat sparked by the arrival of Europeans and the trade they opened with Native Americans. Paul R. Misencik and Sally E. Miscencik, *American Indians of the Ohio Country in the 18th Century* (Jefferson, NC: McFarland, 2020), 24. The tribe also split over the question of Christianity, with those accepting its tenets moving to Montreal and those opposed moving to Ohio.
19. Misencik and Misencik, *American Indians*, 341.
20. Gregory Evans Dowd, *A Spirited Resistance* (Baltimore: Johns Hopkins University Press, 1992), 83; Eric Sterner, *Anatomy of a Massacre: The Destruction of Gnadenhutten, 1782* (Yardley, PA: Westholme, 2020), 111-125. Chippewa is the anglicization of Ojibwe. Eighteenth-century sources used both, as I have here following the source material.
21. Michael N. McConnell, *A Country Between: The Upper Ohio Valley and its Peoples, 1734-1774* (Lincoln: University of Nebraska Press, 1992), 208-210.
22. Eric Sterner, "The Treaty of Fort Pitt, 1778: The First U.S.–American Indian Treaty," *Journal of the American Revolution*, December 18, 2018, accessed January 12, 2023, https://allthingsliberty.com/2018/12/the-treaty-of-fort-pitt-1778-the-first-u-s-american-indian-treaty/.
23. Richard S. Grimes, *The Western Delaware Indian Nation, 1730–1795: Warriors and Diplomats* (Bethlehem, PA: Lehigh University Press, 2017), 208, Kindle.
24. Colin Calloway, *The Indian World of George Washington* (New York: Oxford University Press, 2018), 51.
25. The Mingoes, Shawnese and Delawares to Major DePeyster, June 8, 1782, *Collections and Researches*, 583-584.
26. Rev. Joshua Crawford, "Address on the Crawford Expedition (1782) Delivered Before the Seventh Annual Meeting of the Richland County Historical Society," in *Past and Present of Wyandot County, Ohio*, vol. 1, ed. A. J. Baughman (Chicago: S. J. Clarke Publishing, 1913), 100; Butterfield, *Historical Account*, 166n6. Butterfield thought these numbers high and revised the Delaware count to two hundred and the Wyandot count to less than four hundred, out of a population he believed was only seven hundred. Even this number is high if one believes that warriors constitute no more than one-third of the seven hundred men, women, and children Butterfield believed present on the Sandusky. He later revised the numbers down and made them more vague, conceding only that the Indians totaled "not less than two hundred." Butterfield, *History of the Girtys*, 163.
27. Thompson, *Disaster on the Sandusky*, loc. 3371. Thompson essentially endorses Butterfield's initial estimates.
28. Butterfield, *History of the Girtys*, 163; Hoffman, *Simon Girty*, 165. Hoffman accepts Butterfield's estimate as comprehensive.
29. *The History of Wyandot County Ohio* (Chicago: Leggett, Conaway, 1884), 246; Butterfield, *Historical Account*, 172; Misencik and Misencik, *American Indians*, 343. Ranger Lieutenant Roger Turney estimated the Shawnee contingent at 140. "John Turney to Major A. S. DePeyster, Commanding at Detroit, June 7, 1782," *Washington-Irvine Correspondence*, 368.

30. Withers, *Chronicles*, 357; *History of the Upper Ohio Valley*, vol. 1 (Madison, WI: Brant & Fuller, 1891), 108-109; Fitzpatrick, *Wilderness War*, 562. Fitzpatrick takes the lower number of Indian warriors.

31. John Heckewelder, *A Narrative of the Mission of the United Brethren Among the Delaware and Mohegan Indians* (Philadelphia: McCarty & Davis, 1820), 235-256.

32. "Alex. McKee of the British Indian Department to DePeyster, June 7, 1782," *Washington-Irvine Correspondence*, 370.

33. Butterfield, *Historical Account*, 65-66.

34. Rose, "Journal, Part 2," 295-296.

35. Butterfield, *Historical Account*, 65.

36. Knight, *Narrative*, 4.

37. Rose, "Journal, Part 1," 139.

38. Rose, "Journal, Part 2," 299.

39. Ibid., 300.

40. Ibid., 299.

41. Rose, "Journal, Part 1," 139.

42. Rose, "Journal, Part 2," 300-301.

43. Ibid., 300.

44. Butterfield, *Historical Account*, 75-76; Rose, "Journal, Part 1," 139. The captains associated with this advance are speculative, but the number of men Rose reported in those five companies is close to the number he expected to be sent. Rose and Butterfield differ in the spelling of last names, which was a common problem. Ellis, ed., *History of Fayette County*, 94.

45. Knight, *Narrative*, 5; Butterfield, *Historical Account*, 138-139.

46. Rose, "Journal, Part 2," 312. Rose conflates the entry into Gnadenhutten and New Schoenbrunn in his memoir. I separated them in the text.

47. Rose, "Journal, Part 1," 141.

48. Robert H. Sherrard, *A Narrative of the Wonderful Escape and Dreadful Sufferings of Colonel James Paul* (Cincinnati: Spiller & Gates, 1869), 9. Sherrard interviewed Paul in 1826 and presented this narrative as Paul's own commentary. So it shifts jarringly from third person to first person midparagraph. Paul died in 1841 at eighty-one, making him twenty-two at the time of the campaign and sixty-six during Sherrard's interview.

49. Rose, "Journal, Part 1," 141; Sherrard, *Narrative*, 9.

50. Rose, "Journal, Part 1," 141; Knight, *Narrative*, 5.

51. Rose, "Journal, Part 2," 295.

52. Ibid., 296-297.

53. Jim Piecuh, ed., *Cavalry of the American Revolution* (Yardley, PA: Westholme, 2012). The first two chapters in particular deal with the development and employment of American cavalry, which often acted as scouts and messengers. They had proved of limited tactical value in the hilly and heavily wooded areas of the north but found more traditional roles in the south.

54. Rose, "Journal, Part 1," 142; Rose, "Journal, Part 2," 302-303; Lieut. Rose to Irvine, June 13th, *Washington-Irvine Correspondence*, 369.

55. *The Military History of Ohio* (New York: H. H. Hardesty, 1887), 107.

56. Rose, "Journal, Part 1," 143-144.

57. Butterfield, *Historical Account*, 142.

58. Rose, "Journal, Part 1," 143-145.

59. Ibid., 146.

60. Butterfield, *Historical Account*, 143.

61. Rose, "Journal, Part 1," 147; Knight, *Narrative*, 5-6.

62. Eugene F. Bliss, ed., *Diary of David Zeisberger: A Moravian Missionary among the Indians of Ohio* (Cincinnati: Robert Clarke, 1885), 19-20.

63. Rose, "Journal, Part 1," 148.

64. Ibid.; J. P. MacLean, ed., *Journal of Michael Walters, A Member of the Expedition Against Sandusky in the Year 1782*, tract 89, vol. 4 (Cleveland: Western Reserve Historical Society, 1899), 182. John Beason's last name is sometimes spelled "Beeson," and he appears to have been in the rear guard under Colonel Gattis. The cannon fire itself is one of the battle's unresolved mysteries. To move faster, Caldwell left his small guns behind. On the night of June 5, they were still several miles north of Upper Sandusky. The morning of June 4 was foggy, and fog can have curious acoustical effects, but Johnathan Leith, a trader scurrying north with his wares and cattle who also reported cannon fire, was camped roughly thirty miles north of today's Upper Sandusky while the Americans were several miles south of it. Brown, "Battle of Sandusky," 135-136n57.

CHAPTER 3: BATTLE ISLAND

1. Reuben Gold Thwaites, ed., *A Short Biography of John Leeth with an Account of his Life among the Indians*, reprint (Cleveland: Burrows Brothers, 1904), 41. Johnathan Leith's narrative was taken down and modified by Ewel Jeffries, who misspelled Leith's last name in the narrative's first printing in 1831. It then underwent several reprintings with the misspelling intact. Thwaites, an authority on the frontier war, decided to leave Jeffries's error in the 1904 reprint because that is how it was known to generations. Although the volume was offered as Leith's first person narrative, the words belong to Jeffries. The cannon shots are a mystery of the Crawford campaign. Caldwell apparently left Detroit with two small pieces of horse-portable artillery but decided to leave them at Lower Sandusky. Rose, Walters, and Leith all reported hearing cannon shot on the morning of June 4, but nobody reported being fired on by artillery during the battle.

2. Reuben Thwaites and C. W. Butterfield fleshed out this biography of Leith in their respective introductions and biographies of Leith in two of the narrative reprints. The 1904 reprint contains both, better explaining Jeffries's version of Leith's account.

3. Thwaites, *Short Biography*, 40.

4. Butterfield and Fitzpatrick both place Leith in Upper Sandusky early in the morning of June 4 and meeting Elliott and then Caldwell while he traveled north with his cattle and wares and they traveled south with their reinforcements that morning. That timeline does not sync with the cannon fire Leith and some volunteers reported hearing in the early hours of June 4 or subsequent reports that Elliott or Caldwell were on the field at the opening of the battle. The best explanation for the discrepancy may be that Butterfield simply made a mistake. See also Brown, "Battle of Sandusky," 135-136.

5. Rose, "Journal, Part 1," 148.

6. Brown, "Battle of Sandusky," 136; Butterfield, *Historical Account*, 152-153. Butterfield's route march has the volunteers crossing the Sandusky several times as they moved north, but Brown followed Rose's journal and concluded that the expedition traveled south and then west of the river as it turned north. Butterfield did not have access to Rose's journal at the time his book was published and likely conflated the creek crossings with crossings of the Sandusky, particularly since the guides themselves were often unsure where those creeks ultimately flowed.

7. Rose, "Journal, Part 1," 149. Indications were that the Wyandot had abandoned this town site well before the expedition set out and not in response to the rumors of a pending attack.

8. Brown, "Battle of Sandusky," 137; Rose, "Journal, Part 1," 149.

9. Knight, *Narrative*, 5.

10. Rose, "Journal, Part 1," 149. Rose later blamed "Captain L," leading one of his two companies, for dismounting his men and sheltering them behind trees, weakening the light horse available for the scout. He blamed "H" for the order to fight dismounted. Captain L was probably Captain William Leet and "H" probably Major Harrison. Rose, "Journal, Part 2," 303. Part 2 of Rose's memoir was clearly composed after his journal, and the expatriate baron does a fair amount of axe grinding in it, but he thought other staff members, Majors Leet and Harrison, were undermining his position, ideas, and the command decisions made either by Crawford or his officers councils. Ironically, it is obvious that Rose spent a good portion of his time telling his superior officers their business, even though the expatriate had less experience on the frontier, working with militia or volunteers, and fighting Native Americans.

11. Knight, *Narrative*, 5.

12. Brown, "Battle of Sandusky," 137. Rose ignored this ambush in his memoir. There might be several explanations: it was a modest affair triggered early and not worth mentioning; he was embarrassed by stumbling into it; it did not occur.

13. Rose, "Journal, Part 1," 149.

14. John Turney to Major A. S. DePeyster, Commanding at Detroit, June 7, 1782, *Washington-Irvine Correspondence*, 368. Captain Caldwell, of the Rangers, to DePeyster, June 11, 1782, *Washington-Irvine Correspondence*, 371. The exact timing of Caldwell's arrival at the battlefield may be open to debate. Turney is clear that the rangers were on the field on June 4. On the American side, however, Rose reported their arrival on June 5 with the Shawnee. Lieut. Rose to Irvine, June 13, 1782, *Washington-Irvine Correspondence*, 371. Several subsequent histories of the battle followed Rose, but I am inclined to accept Turney's note at face value. His perspective was plainly clearer, and he wrote his report closer to the time of the battle. The Americans simply might have been slow to realize the ranger presence.

15. Turney to DePeyster, June 7, 1782, *Washington-Irvine Correspondence*, 368. On the American side, volunteer Michael Walters also timed the opening of the battle around 2:00 PM. MacLean, *Journal of Michael Walters*, 182.

16. Rose, "Journal, Part 1," 149-150.

17. Petition of Angus McCoy, Revolutionary War Pension and Bounty-Land Warrant Application Files, National Archives, record no. S22390 (hereafter Petition of Angus McCoy), https://www.fold3.com/image/23855219. McCoy's pension application raises interesting questions about the nature of his participation. McCoy's militia class was called up in the spring, and he served under Captain Swearingen, then was discharged. His brother William's class was called up immediately after, and Angus volunteered for the Crawford campaign in lieu of William's militia service.

18. Rose, "Journal, Part 1," 150.

19. John Turney to Major A. S. DePeyster, Commanding at Detroit, June 7, 1782," *Washington-Irvine Correspondence*, 368.

20. Rose, "Journal, Part 1," 150.

21. Knight, *Narrative*, 6.

22. Rose, "Journal, Part 1," 150; Knight, *Narrative*, 6; Turney to DePeyster, June 7, 1782, *Washington-Irvine Correspondence*, 368.

23. Rose, "Journal, Part 2," 298-299.

24. Petition of Angus McCoy.

25. The quote is from Rose, "Journal, Part 1," 150; Knight, *Narrative*, 6; Turney to DePeyster, June 7, 1782, *Washington-Irvine Correspondence*, 368. Turney reported to DePeyster that the initial engagement involved two hundred Indians plus the British rangers.

26. Rose specifically mentions Brenton on the left and Gattis in the rear, so the assumption is a reasonable one, but it remains an assumption nonetheless.

27. Cruikshank, "Story of Butler's Rangers," in *Butler's Rangers*, 105; Reginald Horsman, *Matthew Elliott, British Indian Agent* (Detroit: Wayne State University Press, 1964), 37; Fitzpatrick, *Wilderness War*, 467. Fitzpatrick cites DePeyster's orders to Caldwell regarding Elliott directing the Indians. Butterfield, *Historical Account*, 178. Despite its limitations, Butterfield's account was the most thorough treatment of the Sandusky campaign for decades, and most subsequent histories followed, or built on, it.

28. Sterner, *Anatomy of a Massacre*, ch. 4. The Moravian removal is an example of the interplay of Anglo and Indian interests on the frontier. Captain Elliott blamed Dunquat for removing the Moravians to the Sandusky; Dunquat blamed Major DePeyster, and DePeyster blamed Hopocan. In truth, all of them had converging, but different, interests and reasons for removing the Moravian missionaries and their Indian congregations from the Muskingum and then separating the missionaries from their converts.

29. Turney to DePeyster, June 7, 1782, *Washington-Irvine Correspondence*, 368. Turney reported that Caldwell's rangers and two hundred Indians "marched out to fight them." See also, Horsman, *Matthew Elliott*, 37; Fitzpatrick, *Wilderness War*, 468-469; Cruikshank, "Story of Butler's Rangers," in *Butler's Rangers*, 104. Cruikshank places the number of Lake Indians at forty-four, but such precise figures were unreliable in any given moment since individuals and small parties would come and go at their own discretion.

30. For Dunquat's dominance, see Sterner, *Anatomy of a Massacre*, ch. 4.

31. Fitzpatrick, *Wilderness War*, 470-471; Horsman, *Matthew Elliott*, 37-38. Fitzpatrick and Horsman credit Elliott with the plan of encirclement, but neither
identifies a source. In truth, Dunquat was already an experienced combat leader,
and encirclement tactics were an oft-used Indian tactic.
32. Sherrard, *Narrative*, 10; Robert Andrew Sherrard and Thomas Johnson Sherrard, eds., *The Sherrard Family of Steubenville Together with Letters, Records and Genealogies of Related Families* (Philadelphia: Jas. N. Rodgers Printing, 1890), 11.
The two Robert Sherrards are the same individual, despite the different middle
initials. Robert Sherrard's father was John Sherrard, who served in Biggs's company. Robert Sherrard also took down a narrative in person from James Paul in
1826, which he turned into a manuscript. The family history was self-published
for the family and is based on family stories and some material Sherrard could
confirm to his own satisfaction, including comments by John Rodgers, who
served on the campaign. There are limitations in Sherrard's retellings of both
stories, which Parker Brown explains at some length. Brown, "Battle of Sandusky," 132-134. The Pennsylvania Archives includes John Sherrard, John
Rodgers, James Paul, and David and John Cannon in the company roster. But,
as discussed elsewhere, the archive rolls are incomplete and often inaccurate
with names. Thomas Lynch Montgomery, ed., *The Pennsylvania Archives*, ser. 6,
vol. 2 (Harrisburg, PA: Harrisburg Publishing, 1906), 386-387. Butterfield and
Brown both repeated the Daniel Canon story, the former engaging in direct
correspondence with Robert Sherrard.
33. Quoted in Butterfield, *Historical Account*, 210. Butterfield heard the quote
second-hand from Robert Sherrard. Sherrard, *Narrative*, 10.
34. Brown, "Battle of Sandusky," 138.
35. Sherrard, *Sherrard Family*, 11; Sherrard, *Narrative*, 10.
36. Alternative spellings for Dunlavy's last name include Dunlevy and Dernboy.
The spelling here is from his pension application. Butterfield, *Historical Account*,
211; *Pennsylvania Archives*, ser. 6, vol. 2, 388; Francis Dunlavy, *Case Files of Pension
and Bounty-Land Warrant Applications Based on Revolutionary War Service*, compiled
ca. 1800–ca. 1912, documenting the period ca. 1775–ca. 1900, Virginia Applications, record 2526. The Pennsylvania Archives roll lists Dunlavy as a lieutenant, but his pension application states he served in the capacity of sergeant.
He was in his seventies at the time of his application.
37. Butterfield, *Historical Account*, 211. Butterfield times this confrontation on
June 4 based on personal communications with family members well after the
war. Those same communications insist that "Big Captain Johnny" was a seven-
foot-tall Shawnee who later joined the Americans during the War of 1812. Three
men were known alternatively as Captain John or Captain Johnny on the frontier about this time, and all three were generally known to be tall: Welapachtsch-
iechen was a Delaware chief who converted to Christianity in 1777 and was
murdered at Gnadenhutten. The Indian whom Dunlavy's kin saw during the
War of 1812 was a Shawnee known only as Captain John, who was described as
"ugly" as he was tall with a nasty mean streak. But he was likely too young to
have participated at the Battle of Sandusky. The third was an older Shawnee
named Kekewepelethy, who was about the right age at the Battle of Sandusky

but died before the War of 1812. It is likely that Dunlavy's family history confused Kekewepelethy with the younger, cruel Captain John and that Butterfield repeated the error in his text.

38. Colin G. Calloway, *The Victory with No Name: The Native American Defeat of the First American Army* (Oxford: Oxford University Press, 2015), 42, Kindle; Adam Jortner, *The Gods of Prophetstown: The Battle of Tippecanoe and the Holy War for the American Frontier* (Oxford: Oxford University Press, 2012), 57; John Sugden, *Bluejacket: Warrior of the Shawnees* (Lincoln: University of Nebraska Press, 2000), 50-51.

39. Hermann Wellenreuther and Carola Wessel, eds., *The Moravian Mission Diaries of David Zeisberger, 1772–1781* (University Park: Pennsylvania State University Press, 2005), 17; Amy C. Schutt, *Peoples of the River Valleys: The Odyssey of the Delaware Indians* (Philadelphia: University of Pennsylvania Press, 2007); C. A. Weslager, *The Delaware Indians: A History* (New Brunswick, NJ: Rutgers University Press, 1972), 308-309; Sugden, *BlueJacket*, 285n2.

40. It is possible that Dunlevy's duel with Kewepelethy took place on June 5, after the bulk of the Shawnee reinforcements arrived. However, most of the fighting that day took place at greater ranges.

41. Butterfield, *Historical Account*, 252-257.

42. Knight, *Narrative*, 6.

43. Brown, "Battle of Sandusky," 138; *Pennsylvania Archives*, ser. 6, vol 2, 396. The archives list William Bready on the roll for Munn's company. The archives also list a William Brady in Captain David Reed's company, but Rose offered no information about that company in his account of the battle. It is more likely that a member of Munn's own company rode to the captain's rescue.

44. Brown, "Battle of Sandusky," 138. *Pennsylvania Archives*, ser. 6, vol. 2, 389, lists Angus and Alexander Mackay in Bilderback's company. Petition of Angus McCoy.

45. Brown, "Battle of Sandusky," 138.

46. Rose, "Journal, Part 1," 150.

47. Knight, *Narrative*, 6.

48. Brown, "Battle of Sandusky," 138-139; *Pennsylvania Archives*, ser. 6, vol. 2, 392.

49. Butterfield, *Historical Account*, 210, 212. Brown, "Battle of Sandusky," 128. Philip Smith does not appear in the published muster rolls from Westmoreland County, but they cover less than half of the volunteers' number. A Philip Smith from Pennsylvania did apply for a Revolutionary War service pension in the 1830s. He claimed to have served at Valley Forge but made no such assertions about the Crawford campaign. His application was denied. The would-be pensioner and Butterfield's Smith may not be the same person. Pennsylvania Pension Application of Philip Smith, R. 9828, https://www.fold3.com/image/16876977.

50. MacLean, "Journal of Michael Walters," 182.

51. Rose, "Journal, Part 2," 303.

52. Rose, "Journal, Part 1," 150-151. The quote is from MacLean, "Journal of Michael Walters," 182.

53. Petition of Angus McCoy. Leet led a similar breakout on June 5, and McCoy's memories of the battle may have confused this event with that one, but his ap-

plication otherwise follows a generally chronological order, and it is reasonable to place this charge on June 4 and connect it to the clearing of the southern skirt of woods near both Gattis's and McClelland's commands.

54. Brown, "Battle of Sandusky," 138; Thompson, *Disaster on the Sandusky*, loc. 3532; Rose, "Journal, Part 2," 293.
55. Rose, "Journal, Part 2," 293.
56. Rose, "Journal, Part 1," 151.
57. Ibid.; Butterfield, *Historical Account*, 212. Butterfield counted five killed and nineteen wounded. Dr. Knight only noted four killed and twenty-three wounded, including seven severely for the entire battle, but he was not the only physician and dictated his narrative several exhausting weeks after the battle.
58. Brown, "Battle of Sandusky," 139.
59. Rose, "Journal, Part 1," 151; Turney to DePeyster, June 7, 1782, *Washington-Irvine Correspondence*, 368; Knight, *Narrative*, 6. Knight reported cannon fire in the predawn hours of June 5, but his narrative was dictated from a hospital bed after weeks of physical exertion and deprivation. No other source reported such fire, and Knight likely erred in his timeline. He was remembering the cannon fire Leith and others reported before dawn on June 4.
60. Rose, "Journal, Part 1," 151; Lieut. Rose to Irvine, June 13, 1782, *Washington-Irvine Correspondence*, 371.
61. Rose, "Journal, Part 1," 151-152.
62. Ibid., 151.
63. Rose, "Journal, Part 2," 306; *Military History of Ohio*, 108.
64. Turney to DePeyster, June 7, 1782, *Washington-Irvine Correspondence*, 368
65. Sherrard, *Sherrard Family*, 12. Sherrard's story falls in the category of family lore, which usually has to be taken with a grain of salt.
66. John Walters Pension Application, 17753, Fold3, https://www.fold3.com/image/19932046. This phrase is often cited, but the wording may have been crafted by the official recording the declaration, made in 1832.
67. Brown, "Battle of Sandusky," 140.
68. Turney to DePeyster, June 7, 1782, *Washington-Irvine Correspondence*, 368. Butterfield and those who followed his lead placed the arrival of the British rangers late in the afternoon of June 5 and the Shawnee that evening. But Turney is clear on the matter that the rangers engaged the Americans on June 4, that Caldwell was wounded early in the action and sent to Lower Sandusky in the evening of June 4, and that the Shawnee arrived around noon on June 5. Hoffman, *Simon Girty*, 169. Hoffman marks James Girty's arrival on the battlefield with the Shawnee.
69. Rose, "Journal, Part 1," 151.
70. MacLean, "Journal of Michael Walters," 183.
71. Rose, "Journal, Part 2," 305.
72. Brown, "Battle of Sandusky," 140n69.
73. Butterfield, *History of the Girtys*, 169-170.
74. Thompson, *Disaster on the Sandusky*, loc. 3636. Thompson takes this story from two recent biographies of Girty: Edward Butts, *Simon Girty: Wilderness Warrior* (Toronto: Dundurn Press, 2011), 144, Kindle, and Hoffman, *Simon Girty*, 169. Butts and Hoffman do not cite their sources for the story.

75. Brown, "Battle of Sandusky," 140n69.

76. Lieut. Rose to Irvine, June 13, 1782, *Washington-Irvine Correspondence*, 371. Unfortunately, Butterfield took those American observations as the rangers' actual time of arrival and subsequent historians followed his lead. Butterfield, *Historical Account*, 216.

77. Quoted in Brown, "Battle of Sandusky," 141n71.

78. Rose, "Journal, Part 1," 151-152.

79. Ibid., 151.

80. Lieut. Rose to Irvine, June 13, 1782, *Washington-Irvine Correspondence*, 372.

81. Sherrard, *Narrative*, 10.

82. Sherrard, *Sherrard Family*, 12. It should be remembered that Robert Sherrard assembled both accounts from family stories and local lore, and the accounts reflect his reconstruction of the battle as much as they resemble first-person narratives.

83. Knight, *Narrative*, 6.

84. Slover, *Narrative*, 17; Brown, "Battle of Sandusky," 141; Thompson, *Disaster on the Sandusky*, loc. 3636-3652.

85. Sherrard, *Narrative*, 11. Sherrard or Paul gets the dates for the entire campaign wrong, placing them a day later than they occurred.

86. Knight, *Narrative*, 6.

87. Rose, "Journal, Part 1," 152. Rose notes the orders chronologically in his diary after he notes the *feu de joie*, but he is not specific about the time those orders were issued.

88. Withers, *Chronicles*, 330. Alexander Withers was born in northwestern Virginia in 1792 and lived most of his life in settlements along the Ohio River. He collected and recorded local stories into a series of newspaper articles, which were eventually bound in a book first published in 1832. Subsequent editions were edited by noted frontier historians Lyman Draper and Reuben Thwaites. The references here are to the text contained in Thwaite's last edition, which is a faithful reprint of the 1832 edition with added commentary and notes. Pagination comes from the 1832 print. Doddridge, *Notes*, 209-210. Like Withers, Doddridge first published his volume as a series of newspaper articles, then self-published them as a bound volume in 1824. Subsequent editions were released after 1876. This is the third edition containing his daughter's notes and memoir of her father, published after her death and including notes added by others in the area covered in the book. Pagination follows the 1912 edition.

89. Butterfield, *Historical Account*, 217-218. Butterfield's case rests on Knight's narrative, which may be more weight than the narrative can carry. Several different councils are also a possibility, as Crawford was constantly moving among his men and presumably consulting with his officers. So the process may have been less formal than an all-hands meeting with the senior officers.

90. Rose, "Journal, Part 1," 152; Knight, *Narrative*, 6.

91. Rose, "Journal, Part 1," 152.

92. Brown, "Battle of Sandusky," 142.

93. Rose, "Journal, Part 1," 152, 308.

94. Rose noted that the firing began shortly after Hardin's departure.

95. Rose, "Journal, Part 1," 152; Slover, *Narrative*, 17; Brown, "Battle of Sandusky," 142.
96. Rose, "Journal, Part 2," 309; MacLean, "Journal of Michael Walters," 183.
97. Rose, "Journal, Part 1," 152; Brown, "Battle of Sandusky," 142-143.
98. Sherrard, *Narrative*, 11-12.
99. Slover, *Narrative*, 17-18.
100. Sherrard, *Narrative*, 12-13.
101. Brown, "Battle of Sandusky," 145.
102. Ibid.
103. Ibid., 143-144. See especially notes 74 and 76. Brown reviews the historiography concerning Leet's role and sudden disappearance from the campaign after Brenton's men broke through. Because Leet and the troops he led did not rejoin the largest group of volunteers, Rose's estimation of the veteran may have fallen.
104. Scholl, *Brothers Crawford*, 1:48.
105. Knight, *Narrative*, 7.
106. Ibid.
107. Petition of Angus McCoy.
108. Ibid. Taking the wrong road serves as the foundation of putting McCoy and Rose together, which Brown does. Brown, "Battle of Sandusky," 145.
109. Rose, "Journal, Part 1," 152.
110. Butterfield, *Historical Account*, 225; Rose, "Journal, Part 1," 153.
111. Petition of Angus McCoy; Rose, "Journal, Part 1," 153; Butterfield, *Historical Account*, 233; Brown, "Battle of Sandusky," 146.
112. Brown, "Battle of Sandusky," 136, 146. Brown indicates a ranger scalped Hays. Angus McCoy Petition. McCoy, who observed the event, reported Indians did it. Rose, "Journal, Part 1," 154. Rose also reported that Hays had been shot on Tuesday and identifies the "Yagers," i.e., rangers, as Hays's assailants. He spelled the boy's last name Hayes.
113. Butterfield, *Historical Account*, 226-227. Sherrard, *Sherrard Family*, 14-15. Sherrard left his good saddle at home because it had fallen to him to carry much of the company's flour, for which a packsaddle was more appropriate.
114. Brown, "Battle of Sandusky," 146; Rose, "Journal, Part 1," 153. Henry's status is not entirely clear. Whether that was his first or last name is unknown. Officers often had personal servants to assist with their kit, and a baron might expect one, even in exile. Among Revolutionary War officers, such individuals could be enslaved men. Rose refers to him simply as "Waiter."
115. Rose, "Journal, Part 1," 154.
116. Butterfield, *Historical Account*, 222.
117. Rose, "Journal, Part 2," 309.
118. Turney to DePeyster, June 7, 1782, *Washington-Irvine Correspondence*, 368; Brown, "Battle of Sandusky," 146.
119. Petition of Angus McCoy; Rose, "Journal, Part 1," 153-154.
120. Brown, "Battle of Sandusky," 146-147; Rose, "Journal, Part 2," 310.
121. Butterfield, *Historical Account*, 235-236. Turney and Caldwell both reported a French interpreter named LeVillier being killed during the multiday battle. Butterfield connects their LeVillier with Leith's Frenchman. The story about

LeVillier painting the target on his chest was contained in a private communication between William Walker and A. H. Dunlavy, who passed it on to Butterfield. Walker was a young resident of the area in the early 1800s who claimed to know Simon Girty and reportedly visited several of the relevant sites with elderly Wyandot warriors and leaders. Butterfield, who also lived in the area, became acquainted with Walker in the latter's old age. So the story was handed down verbally over three generations before Butterfield recorded it.

122. Rose, "Journal, Part 1," 153.

123. Brown, "Battle of Sandusky," 146-147; Rose, "Journal, Part 1," 153-154; Petition of Angus McCoy; Butterfield, *Historical Account*, 237.

124. Rose, "Journal, Part 2," 311.

125. Thompson, *Disaster on the Sandusky*, loc. 3736.

126. Rose, "Journal, Part 1," 153-154. Angus McCoy reported in his pension application that Hays's wounds were mortal but that he survived several days after the Battle of Olentangy. So his remaining behind on the seventh may have had more to do with his wounds than baking bread.

127. Sherrard, *Sherrard Family*, 15. Most of Sherrard's dates are off by twenty-four hours, but his chronology seems to synchronize about this time, the evening of June 7.

128. Rose, "Journal, Part 1," 156.

129. Col. David Williamson to Irvine, June 13, 1782, *Washington-Irvine Correspondence*, 366-367.

130. Lieut. Rose to Irvine, June 13, 1782, *Washington-Irvine Correspondence*, 367-378; Rose, "Journal, Part 1," 156. In his June 13 letter report to Irvine, Rose estimated losses of thirty killed and wounded, later increasing that number in his more thorough journal.

131. Turney to DePeyster, June 7, 1782, *Washington-Irvine Correspondence*, 368; Same to Same, June 7, 1782, *Washington-Irvine Correspondence*, 369.

132. Alex McKee of the British Indian Department to DePeyster, June 7, 1782, *Washington-Irvine Correspondence*, 370.

133. Speech of Captain Snake on Behalf of the Mingoes, Shawanese and Delawares to DePeyster, June 8[7], 1782, *Washington-Irvine Correspondence*, 369-370.

134. Fitzpatrick, *Wilderness War*, 486-487; Captain William Caldwell, of the Rangers, to DePeyster, June 11, 1782, *Washington-Irvine Correspondence*, 372.

135. DePeyster to Thomas Brown, Superintendent of Indian Affairs, July 18, 1782, *Washington-Irvine Correspondence*, 372; Gen. Haldimand to Sir Guy Carleton, July 28, 1782, *Washington-Irvine Correspondence*, 373.

CHAPTER 4: EXECUTIONS AND ESCAPES

1. Historian Parker Brown believes that the younger man, whom Dr. Knight did not name, was likely Private Hanes Mitchell of Captain Biggs's company. Parker Brown, "The Historical Accuracy of the Captivity Narrative of Doctor John Knight," *Western Pennsylvania Historical Magazine* 70, no. 1 (January 1987): 60.

2. Brown believed that Knight's "Lieutenant Ashley" was Ensign Hankers Ashby of Captain's Dean's company under Colonel Gattis, assigned to the rear body. Westmoreland County rolls for the campaign, however, include Lieutenant

Thomas Ashley in Captain Andrew Hood's company, which was assigned to the left under Brenton. The uncertainty is the result of some of the more vague aspects of Knight's narrative, the doctor's own unfamiliarity with some of the men, poor record keeping, and general disorganization on the night of June 5-6. The Westmoreland County rolls indicate that Lieutenant Ashley was wounded, captured, and burned during the campaign. Because Knight's account syncs with the volunteer rolls, I am more inclined to believe that Knight's Lieutenant Ashley was in fact Thomas Ashley.

3. Knight, *Narrative*, 8.
4. Ibid.
5. Ibid., 9.
6. Brown, "Historical Accuracy," 60.
7. MacLean, "Journal of Michael Walters," 183.
8. This clearly calls into question Walters's estimate of the distance they had traveled.
9. Brown, "Historical Accuracy," 60; MacLean, "Journal of Michael Walters," 183.
10. Brown identifies these Indians as Chippewa. Brown, "Historical Accuracy," 60.
11. MacLean, "Journal of Michael Walters," 184.
12. Hoffman, *Simon Girty*, 4-9; Butts, *Simon Girty*, 21-24, Kindle.
13. Hoffman, *Simon Girty*, 16-19. Thomas Girty's situation at this time is unclear. He may have been rescued during the raid or otherwise escaped from the Delaware after arriving at the village. Butterfield, *History of the Girtys*, 13-15.
14. Butts, *Simon Girty*, 41.
15. Ibid., 64-66.
16. Hoffman, *Simon Girty*, 84; Butts, *Simon Girty*, 67.
17. Sterner, "General Edward Hand."
18. Hoffman, *Simon Girty*, 98-100.
19. Knight, *Narrative*, 9.
20. Hoffman, *Simon Girty*, 171.
21. Ibid.; Brown, "Historical Accuracy," 60-61; Butterfield, *History of the Girtys*, 173. Butterfield traces the source of the reward offer to a Moravian Indian who allegedly overheard the conversation, and the origins of the offer to reveal military intelligence to Simon Girty himself. He discounts the reward offer, arguing that Girty never mentioned it but that Girty did report Crawford's offer to reveal secrets.
22. Hoffman, *Simon Girty*, 316n2.
23. Butterfield, *Historical Account*, 199.
24. Hoffman's book is the standard modern biography. It is well cited but generally uses the same source material as Brown and Butterfield. Butts's short biography largely follows Hoffman.
25. Knight, *Narrative*, 9-10; Brown, "Historical Accuracy," 61.
26. Slover, *Narrative*, 18.
27. Sherrard, *Narrative*, 13. Paul thought the stop occurred around noon.
28. Ibid., 13-14; Slover, *Narrative*, 18.
29. Slover, *Narrative*, 18, 19; Sherrard, *Narrative*, 15-16.
30. Slover, *Narrative*, 19. Slover's reference to "chargers" in this case is not to horses, as the men were afoot. It refers to a device used to load muskets. See,

for example, Richard M. Lederer Jr., *Colonial American English* (Essex, CT: Verbatim, 1985), 47.

31. Slover, *Narrative*, 19.
32. Sherrard, *Narrative*, 16-17.
33. Slover, *Narrative*, 21.
34. Ibid., 21-22, 23.
35. Knight, *Narrative*, 10.
36. Ibid., 10, 14.
37. Brown, "Historical Accuracy," 61.
38. Doddridge, *Notes*, 212. For decades after the events, Americans tended to simply repeat what Knight and Doddridge had recorded. See, for example, Withers, *Chronicles*, 333; Butterfield, *History of the Girtys*, 173-175; *History of Wyandot County*, 252; and William Hintzen, *Border Wars of the Upper Ohio Valley, 1769–1794* (Ashland, KY: Jesse Stuart Foundation, 2011), 188.
39. Hoffman, *Simon Girty*, 172.
40. Heckewelder, *Narrative of the Mission*, 339-340. Heckewelder was a missionary who lived among the Moravian Indians on the Muskingum. Many of his parishioners were killed in the massacre. By the time of the Crawford campaign, DePeyster had forcibly removed the Moravian missionaries from their congregations on the Sandusky at the behest of Hopocan and Simon Girty. But Heckewelder had deep connections to and experiences with those who remained behind, whether they had joined his church or not.
41. Brown, "Historical Accuracy," 61.
42. Hoffman, *Simon Girty*, 173.
43. Horsman, *Matthew Elliott*, 39; Hoffman, *Simon Girty*, 173-174.
44. Brown, "Historical Accuracy," 61.
45. Hoffman, *Simon Girty*, 173.
46. DePeyster to Thomas Brown, Superintendent of Indian Affairs, July 18, 1782, *Washington-Irvine Correspondence*, 372. Matthew Elliott's name was inserted in the brackets by C. W. Butterfield, the volume's editor.
47. Knight, *Narrative*, 11. There are reports that between the council meeting and Crawford being tied to the pole, the colonel spoke with Wingenund, with whom he had once been friendly. Crawford reportedly asked the chief to intercede, but Wingenund demurred, pointing out that Crawford's association with Williamson and his own actions had brought the American to this place. Butterfield attributes the story to Heckewelder, who may have heard it from Wingenund, but is not inclined to accept Heckewelder's version. Neither provides sufficient sourcing to track down the story. Such an exchange makes more sense as part of the council meeting, in which Crawford attempted to defend himself. Heckewelder, *Narrative of the Mission*, 339; *Military History of Ohio*, 108; Butterfield, *Historical Account*, 382-383.
48. Knight, *Narrative*, 11-12.
49. Hoffman, *Simon Girty*, 175. The source is again Girty's daughter.
50. Brown, "Historical Accuracy," 62n31.
51. Knight, *Narrative*, 12-13. The Delaware who took Crawford's scalp was a convert to the Moravian faith and had taken the Christian name Joseph. David Zeis-

berger, the senior missionary on the Muskingum who baptized Joseph at Gnadenhutten in 1774, described him as going in "a bad way" virtually from the moment he joined the church. Joseph died in 1788 and received a Christian burial. Bliss, *Diary of David Zeisberger*, 431.

52. Knight, *Narrative*, 12; Heckewelder, *Narrative of the Mission*, 342.

53. Knight, *Narrative*, 13.

54. Ibid., 13.

55. To George Washington from William Irvine, 11 July 1782, *Founders Online*, National Archives, https://founders.archives.gov/documents/Washington/99-01-02-08909.

56. These events and those that follow about Slover's experiences are from Slover, *Narrative*, 23-29.

57. These two campaigns eventually culminated in the Battle of Blue Licks in August and the Siege of Fort Henry in September. Slover also reports directions from Detroit to take no more prisoners, as provisions there were low and it was getting difficult to feed them. The implication was to kill or enslave everyone who fell into Indian hands. This may have been inserted by the narrative's editor, H. H. Brackenridge. Slover assumed that the Indians would change their plans when he escaped, although they did not.

58. Again, this was the western branch of the Muskingum, known now as the Walhonding, not the eastern branch, since named the Tuscarawas, on which sat the Moravian villages burned in March.

59. Sherrard, *Narrative*, 20-22.

CONCLUSION

1. From George Washington to William Irvine, 6 August 1782, *Founders Online*, National Archives, https://founders.archives.gov/documents/Washington/99-01-02-09045.

2. DePeyster to Thomas Brown, Superintendent Of Indian Affairs, July 18, 1782, *Washington-Irvine Correspondence*, 372.

3. Gen. Haldimand to Sir Guy Carleton, July 28, 1782, *Washington-Irvine Correspondence*, 373.

4. Letter of Henry Hamilton to Monsieur ? at the Illinois, circa Dec. 1777, Kathrine Wagner Seineke, *The George Rogers Clark Adventure in the Illinois* (New Orleans: Polyanthos, 1981), 211-212.

5. Irvine to Washington, July 11, 1782, *Washington-Irvine Correspondence*, 128.

6. Irvine to Lincoln, July 1, 1782, *Washington-Irvine Correspondence*, 174-175.

7. People living around Pittsburgh were not alone in the sentiment. George Rogers Clark had his eyes on Detroit as the source of British power on the frontier virtually from the beginning of his Illinois Campaign and frequently tried to work with Continental authorities at Pittsburgh and/or Virginia authorities to take the frontier war north and west. To the frustration of Clark and commanders at Pittsburgh, Continental and state authorities in Virginia and Pennsylvania lacked the resources to launch such a two-pronged campaign.

8. Parker B. Brown, "'Crawford's Defeat': A Ballad," *Western Pennsylvania Historical Magazine* 64, no. 4 (October 1981).

Bibliography

Allen, Thomas B. *Tories: Fighting for the King in America's First Civil War.* New York: Harper, 2010.

Baughman, A. J., ed. *Past and Present of Wyandot County, Ohio.* Vol. 1. Chicago: S. J. Clarke, 1913.

Bliss, Eugene F., ed. *Diary of David Zeisberger: A Moravian Missionary among the Indians of Ohio.* Cincinnati: Robert Clarke, 1885.

Boatner, Mark, III. *Encyclopedia of the American Revolution.* 3rd ed. Mechanicsburg, PA: Stackpole Books, 1994.

Brown, Parker B. "The Battle of Sandusky: June 4–6, 1782." *Western Pennsylvania Historical Magazine* 65, no. 2 (April 1982): 115-151.

———. "'Crawford's Defeat': A Ballad." *Western Pennsylvania Historical Magazine* 62, no. 4 (October 1981): 311-327.

———. "The Historical Accuracy of the Captivity Narrative of Doctor John Knight." *Western Pennsylvania Historical Magazine* 70, no. 1 (January 1987): 53-67.

———. "The Search for the Colonel William Crawford Burn Site: An Investigative Report." *Western Pennsylvania Historical Magazine* 68, no. 1 (January 1985): 43-66.

Butler's Rangers: Three Accounts of the American War of Independence: The Story of Butler's Rangers and the Settlement of Niagara by Ernest Cruikshank; The Story of Cherry Valley by Henry U. Swinnerton;

Wyoming Valley a Sketch of Its Early Annals by Isaac A. Chapman. Np: Oakpast, 2011.

Butterfield, Consul Wilshire. *An Historical Account of the Expedition against Sandusky under Col. William Crawford in 1782.* Cincinnati: Robert Clarke, 1873.

———. *History of the Girtys: Being a Concise Account of the Girty Brothers.* Cincinnati: Robert Clarke, 1890. Reprint, Columbus, OH: Long's College Book Co., 1950.

———, ed. *The Washington-Crawford Letters, Being the Correspondence of George Washington and William Crawford, from 1767 to 1781, Concerning Western Lands.* Cincinnati: Robert Clarke, 1877.

———, ed. *Washington-Irvine Correspondence: The Official Letters Which Passed Between Washington and Brig.-Gen. William Irvine and Between Irvine and Others Concerning Military Affairs in the West from 1781 to 1783.* Madison, WI: David Atwood, 1882.

Butts, Edward. *Simon Girty: Wilderness Warrior.* Toronto: Dundurn Press, 2011. Kindle.

Calloway, Colin G. *The Indian World of George Washington.* New York: Oxford University Press, 2018.

———. *The Victory with No Name: The Native American Defeat of the First American Army.* Oxford: Oxford University Press, 2015. Kindle.

Collections and Researches Made by the Pioneer and Historical Society of the State of Michigan. Vol 10. Lansing, MI: Thorp & Godfrey, State Printers and Binders, 1888.

Crumrine, Boyd, ed. *History of Washington County, Pennsylvania, with Biographical Sketches of Many of its Pioneers and Prominent Men.* Philadelphia: L. H. Everts, 1882.

David, James Corbett. *Dunmore's New World: The Extraordinary Life of a Royal Governor in Revolutionary America.* Charlottesville: University of Virginia Press, 2013. Kindle.

De Hass, Wills. *History of the Early Settlement and Indian Wars of Western Virginia.* Wheeling, VA: H. Hoblitzsell, 1851.

Doddridge, Joseph. *Notes on the Settlement and Indian Wars of the Western Parts of Virginia and Pennsylvania from 1763 to 1783.* Pittsburgh: John S. Ritenour and Wm. T. Lindsey, 1912.

Dowd, Gregory Evans. *A Spirited Resistance*. Baltimore: Johns Hopkins University Press, 1992.

Ellis, Franklin, ed. *History of Fayette County, Pennsylvania with Biographical Sketches of Many of its Pioneers and Prominent Men*. Philadelphia: L. H. Everts, 1882.

Fitzpatrick. Alan. *Wilderness War on the Ohio*. New rev. 2nd ed. Benwood, WV: Fort Henry Publications, 2005.

Founders Online. National Archives.

Grimes, Richard S. *The Western Delaware Indian Nation, 1730–1795: Warriors and Diplomats*. Bethlehem, PA: Lehigh University Press, 2017. Kindle.

Hassler, Edgar W. *Old Westmoreland: A History of Western Pennsylvania during the Revolution*. Pittsburgh: J. R. Weldin, 1900.

Heckewelder, John. *A Narrative of the Mission of the United Brethren Among the Delaware and Mohegan Indians*. Philadelphia: McCarty & Davis, 1820.

Hintzen, William. *Border Wars of the Upper Ohio Valley (1769–1794)*. Ashland, KY: Jesse Stuart Foundation, 2011.

History of the Upper Ohio Valley. Vol. 1. Madison, WI: Brant & Fuller, 1891.

The History of Wyandot County Ohio. Chicago: Leggett, Conaway, 1884.

Hoffman, Philip W. *Simon Girty: Turncoat Hero*. Franklin, TN: Flying Camp Press, 2008.

Horsman, Reginald. *Matthew Elliott, British Indian Agent*. Detroit: Wayne State University Press, 1964.

Jortner, Adam. *The Gods of Prophetstown: The Battle of Tippecanoe and the Holy War for the American Frontier*. Oxford: Oxford University Press, 2012.

Kellogg, Louise Phelps, ed. *Frontier Retreat on the Upper Ohio, 1779–1781*. Draper Series, vol. 5. Madison, WI: State Historical Society of Wisconsin, 1917.

Lederer, Richard M., Jr. *Colonial American English*. Essex, CT: Verbatim, 1985.

Maclean, J. P., ed. *Journal of Michael Walters, a Member of the Expedition Against Sandusky in the Year 1782*. Tract 89, vol. 4. Cleveland: Western Reserve Historical Society, 1899.

McConnell, Michael N. *A Country Between: The Upper Ohio Valley and Its Peoples, 1734–1774.* Lincoln: University of Nebraska Press, 1992.

The Military History of Ohio. New York: H. H. Hardesty, 1887.

Misencik, Paul R., and Sally E. Misencik. *American Indians of the Ohio Country in the 18th Century.* Jefferson, NC: McFarland, 2020. Kindle.

Montgomery, Thomas Lynch, ed. *The Pennsylvania Archives.* Ser. 6, vol. 2. Harrisburg, PA: Harrisburg Publishing, 1906.

Narratives of a Late Expedition against the Indians; With An Account of the Barbarous Execution of Col. Crawford; and The Wonderful Escape of Dr. Knight and John Slover from Captivity, in 1782. Philadelphia: Francis Bailey, 1783.

Nelson, Larry. *A Man of Distinction among Them: Alexander McKee and the Ohio Country Frontier, 1754–1799.* Kent, OH: Kent State University Press, 2000.

Newland, Samuel J. *The Pennsylvania Militia: Defending the Commonwealth and the Nation 1669–1870.* Annville: Commonwealth of Pennsylvania, Department of Military and Veterans Affairs, 2002.

On-Line Institute for Advanced Loyalist Studies. http://www.royalprovincial.com/index.htm.

Pencak, William A., Christian B. Keller, and Barbara A. Gannon, eds. *Pennsylvania: A Military History.* Yardley, PA: Westholme, 2016.

Pennsylvania Archives. 3rd series, vol. 7. Harrisburg, PA: Secretary of the Commonwealth, printed by Clarence M. Busch, 1896.

Piecuh, Jim, ed. *Cavalry of the American Revolution.* Yardley, PA: Westholme, 2012.

Pieper, Thomas L., and James B. Gibney. *Fort Laurens, 1778–1779: The Revolutionary War in Ohio.* Kent, OH: Kent State University Press, 1976.

Richter, Daniel K. *Before the Revolution: America's Ancient Past.* Cambridge, MA: Harvard University Press, 2011. Kindle.

Rose, John. "Journal of a Volunteer Expedition to Sandusky, from May 24 to June 13, 1782, Part 1." Edited by William L. Stone.

Pennsylvania Magazine of History and Biography 18, January 1, 1894.

———. "Journal of a Volunteer Expedition to Sandusky, from May 24 to June 13, 1782, Part 2." Edited by William L. Stone. *Pennsylvania Magazine of History and Biography* 18, 1894.

Scholl, Allen W. *The Brothers Crawford: Colonel William, 1722–1782 and Valentine Jr., 1724–1777.* 2 vols. Berwyn Heights, MD: Heritage Books, 2016.

Schutt, Amy C. *Peoples of the River Valleys: The Odyssey of the Delaware Indians.* Philadelphia: University of Pennsylvania Press, 2007.

Seineke, Kathrine Wagner. *The George Rogers Clark Adventure in the Illinois.* New Orleans: Polyanthos, 1981.

Seymour, Joseph. *The Pennsylvania Associators, 1747–1777.* Yardley, PA: Westholme, 2012.

Sherrard, Robert Andrew, and Thomas Johnson Sherrard, eds. *The Sherrard Family of Steubenville Together with Letters, Records and Genealogies of Related Families.* Philadelphia: Jas. B. Rodgers Printing, 1890.

Sherrard, Robert H. *A Narrative of the Wonderful Escape and Dreadful Sufferings of Colonel James Paul, after the Defeat of Colonel Crawford.* Cincinnati: Spiller & Gates, 1869.

Sterner, Eric. "General Edward Hand: The Squaw Campaign." *Emerging Revolutionary War Era* (blog), March 9, 2018. Accessed December 22, 2022. https://emergingrevolutionarywar.org/2018/03/09/general-edward-hand-the-squaw-campaign/.

———. "The Siege of Fort Laurens, 1778–1779." *Journal of the American Revolution*, December 17, 2019. Accessed December 20, 2022. https://allthingsliberty.com/2019/12/the-siege-of-fort-laurens-1778-1779/.

———. "The Treaty of Fort Pitt, 1778: The First U.S.-American Indian Treaty." *Journal of the American Revolution*, December 18, 2018. Accessed December 22, 2022. https://allthingsliberty.com/2018/12/the-treaty-of-fort-pitt-1778-the-first-u-s-american-indian-treaty/.

Sugden, John. *Bluejacket: Warrior of the Shawnees.* Lincoln: University of Nebraska Press, 2000.

Thompson, Robert N. *Disaster on the Sandusky: The Life of Colonel William Crawford.* Staunton, VA: American History Press, 2017.

Thwaites, Reuben Gold. ed. *A Short Biography of John Leeth with an Account of his Life among the Indians,* reprint. Cleveland: Burrows Brothers, 1904.

Verenna, Thomas. "Explaining Pennsylvania's Militia." *Journal of the American Revolution,* June 17, 2014. Accessed April 13, 2021. https://allthingsliberty.com/2014/06/explaining-pennsylvanias-militia/.

Wellenreuther, Hermann, and Carola Wessel, eds. *The Moravian Mission Diaries of David Zeisberger, 1772–1781.* University Park: Pennsylvania State University Press, 2005.

Weslager, C. A. *The Delaware Indians: A History.* New Brunswick, NJ: Rutgers University Press, 1972.

Williams, Glenn F. *Dunmore's War: The Last Conflict of America's Colonial Era.* Yardley, PA: Westholme, 2017.

———. *Year of the Hangman: George Washington's Campaign against the Iroquois.* Yardley, PA: Westholme, 2005.

Wimer, James. *Events in Indian History.* Lancaster: G. Hills, 1841.

Withers, Alexander Scott. *Chronicles of Border Warfare, or a History of the Settlement by Whites of North Western Virginia, and of the Indian Wars and Massacres in that Section of the State.* Edited by Reuben Gold Thwaites. Cincinnati: Stewart & Kidd, 1912, new edition.

Acknowledgments

ONCE UPON A TIME I THOUGHT WRITING was solitary work. Instead, I have learned that a finished project usually benefits from many hands, sets of eyes, thoughtful ideas, and blunt comments. Like *Anatomy of a Massacre*, to which *The Battle of Upper Sandusky* might serve as sequel, this book profited from the involvement of several people whom I need to thank.

Bruce H. Franklin at Westholme Publishing is a publishing marvel. I had to pack up all my books in the middle of writing and decided to take an impromptu, back-of-the-envelope survey of Westholme titles in my library. They constituted one of the largest percentages of all publishers and were among the highest quality. It is a real honor that Bruce supported my efforts to explore the American Revolution across the Appalachian frontier. This book is better because of his involvement.

Mark Lender and James Kirby Martin, co-editors of Westholme's Small Battles Series, agreed to take this project on, and it benefitted mightily from their practiced eyes as historians, writers, and editors. The campaign has been in the back of my mind for about six years, since I stumbled across Dr. John Knight's account of Colonel William Crawford's execution and Knight's escape. Indirectly, the story compelled me to write *Anatomy of a Massacre*, which is more of a social and political history of the events that led to the butchery. A military history of the Crawford campaign struck me as a natural follow-up, but it didn't quite fit anywhere until Bruce, Mark, and James unveiled the Small Battles Series. Under their guidance, the final product is much stronger.

In 2018, my brother, Dave Sterner, and I were fortunate to visit the area around Wyandot County, Ohio. Ron Marvin of the county historical society introduced us to Tom Hill, who graciously gave us a tour of monuments and sites associated with the Crawford campaign, including the most likely location for Battle Island and the fold in the ground where Lieutenant John Rose's reconnaissance mission was ambushed on June 4, and the possible locations for Crawford's execution. Over the centuries, modern agriculture has changed western Ohio's topography, draining bogs, rerouting creeks, and flattening some hills. Crops have replaced grasslands, but the area still has the open feel that Crawford and the volunteers experienced as they rode west. Tom's encyclopedic knowledge of the area and campaign were invaluable.

Gabe Neville, who writes frequently about the American Revolution on the frontier, kindly read the manuscript as it neared completion, not only offering his valuable thoughts about its organization and clarity but also catching the kinds of errors that embarrass an author. I owe him my appreciation for both.

Ron Silverman tackled the arduous task of copyediting and had to put up with my stylistic quirks. The final product is much improved because of his involvement and contributions. I also owe Tracy Dungan my thanks for his work on the maps and skills in turning my own amateur efforts into something useful for a reader. The Wyandot County Historical Society graciously gave me permission to reproduce the Frank Halbedel paintings, and Ron Marvin worked with Katelyn Muraleetharan of Ohio History Connection to obtain the digital images. My thanks to Ron, the Wyandot County Historical Society, and Katelyn, for their assistance and important work. The Wyandot County Museum proudly displays both original paintings and has a wealth of exhibits explaining local history over the centuries.

Thanks are always due to Don Hagist, editor of the *Journal of the American Revolution,* and Rob Orrison and Phil Greenwalt, co-founders of *Emerging Revolutionary War Era.* They've given me writing homes to explore the Revolution, including the trans-Appalachian theater and constantly teach me new things in their own work.

Finally, I have to thank my family, starting with my brother, Dave, who first listened to the story during our road trip; my daughters, Abigail and Nicole, who patiently listened to the latest developments while I studied the campaign; and my wife, Suzy, without whose love and support this work would not be possible. As always, any remaining errors are mine.

Index

170

INDEX

INDEX